Shadow Work

Identify, Confront, and Transform Your Inner Darkness

Jas Renard

Contents

Introduction

We all have light and darkness inside of us. As children, we freely expressed every aspect of our personalities - joy, sadness, curiosity, anger, love. But over time, we learned to edit ourselves. Our parents, teachers, and society rewarded certain traits and punished others. Qualities like kindness, intelligence, and talent were celebrated. But anger, sexuality, selfishness or other "undesirable" parts were scolded, shamed, and suppressed.

So we locked up those forbidden pieces of ourselves. We hid them away out of fear, anxiety and social conditioning. But our shadow selves don't just disappear. Like pressing on an inflated ball underwater, the harder we push them down, the stronger they push back up.

Our shadows are always with us, lurking beneath our polite exteriors, waiting to surge forth. Have you ever shocked yourself with an outburst of rage over a minor annoyance? Or been surprised by your jealousy over a friend's success? These are signs your shadow is leaking out.

We all have a darker side. It contains the parts of ourselves that we deny or feel ashamed of. But our shadows also hold great power - untapped gifts, unexpressed desires, and latent potential. Engaging with our shadows is the key to becoming whole.

The Swisspsychologist Carl Jung (1875 – 1961) used the term ' shadow ' to refer to a person ' s dark-side,or in other words, the part of their psyche they are not comfortable with, and do not accept as being okay. Jung understood that we all wear masks - personas we present to the world. Our shadows are the flipside of those masks - the messy, imperfect, authentic parts of ourselves.

Jung saw that befriending our shadows was essential for personal growth. He knew that self-acceptance and fulfillment requires embracing the entirety of who we are - shadows and all.

The benefits of shadow work extend far beyond individual well-being. Doing the inner work to confront our own darkness makes us more compassionate towards others. It helps prevent projecting our shadows onto people and situations. Integrating our full selves allows us to have healthier relationships and make a positive difference in the world.

So what exactly is shadow work? It is the ongoing practice of illuminating the darker aspects of our psyches. Just as a shadow takes shape when light hits an object, by shining an inner light on the messy parts of ourselves, we begin to understand them.

Shadow work involves several steps:

1. *Becoming aware of our shadows* - Recognizing those disowned pieces we try to hide, deny or suppress.

2. *Exploring the shadow's origins-* Digging into when and why we began disowning certain parts of ourselves.

3. *Seeing values in our shadows* - Finding the gifts, powers and

positives within our darkness.

4. *Integrating the shadow self* - Embracing our full selves, shadows and all.

Shadow work is a courageous path that promises freedom, authenticity and wholeness. When we disown parts of ourselves, we remain fractured and divided. But when we cultivate compassionate awareness of our shadows, we integrate those exiled pieces and become more complete.

This leads to profound self-understanding and self-acceptance. We come home to ourselves. There is no longer a need to pretend to be perfect - our flaws and vulnerabilities are embraced rather than denied. We find meaning and power in the parts of ourselves we once deemed bad or unacceptable.

The journey into our inner darkness is not always comfortable. Shining a light on shameful memories or destructive impulses takes bravery. We may be tempted to turn away. But facing our shadows is the only way to transmute old wounds and traumas into sources of strength. In this way, shadow work is ultimately an act of self-love.

Integrating our shadows allows us to live with authenticity. We develop true intimacy in relationships when we can show all of who we are. We interact with the world from a place of wholeness rather than inner conflict. Every part of us is honored.

Owning our personal shadows also prevents dark projections onto others. When we are ignorant of our own darkness, we see it everywhere outside ourselves. We spot flaws in others that really reflect our own interior shadows. This leads to intolerance, prejudice and conflict. But when we boldly explore our inner darkness, we perceive reality more clearly.

On the collective level, shadow work is the remedy for polarization, tribalism and "othering." The more we judge different groups as sinister or dangerous, the more we deny our own societal shadows. From income inequality to racism to environmental harm, we must acknowledge our collective shadows before positive change can occur.

Shadow work invites us on a hero's journey towards wholeness. It takes courage to confront our inner demons, but the rewards are life-changing. We break free from fear and shame to embody our full potential. We connect to our sacred, eternal essence that exists beyond all masks and personas. Our darkest spaces become fertile ground for creativity, joy and transcendence. Let us step boldly into the shadows and reclaim our authentic power.

The Origins of Shadow Work

The practice of shadow work has its roots in the pioneering work of Carl Jung, the influential Swiss psychiatrist who founded analytical psychology. Jung's extensive study of the human psyche led him to develop several groundbreaking theories that have become foundational in psychology and psychotherapy.

Central to Jung's model of the psyche are four key components: the persona, shadow, anima/animus, and Self. The persona represents our public mask - how we present ourselves to others. In contrast, the shadow symbolizes the parts of ourselves we repress, deny or deem unacceptable. The anima and animus embody the feminine and masculine energies within us all. And the Self signifies our whole, integrated psyche encompassing both conscious and unconscious elements.

Defining the Shadow Self

Most relevant to shadow work is Jung's conception of the shadow. He believed we all have a dark side composed of buried memories, undesirable impulses, weaknesses and latent potentials we reject. This shadow self forms as a counterbalance to the persona - our polished social facade.

So what exactly comprises this mysterious, unseen shadow self? Simply put, it is the collection of all the parts of ourselves that we don't want to or can't face. The shadow represents our inner darkness—those aspects of our personality that we repress, deny, devalue, or feel ashamed of.

We all have flaws, weaknesses, vulnerabilities, embarrassing memories, and impulses that don't align with who we think we are or who we want to present to the world. Society, family upbringing, and traumatic experiences all contribute to behaviors, emotions, desires, and attributes we learn to reject. We instinctively hide these away in the shadows.

The shadow self can contain a laundry list of unsavory disowned traits: fury, hatred, greed, selfishness, violence, lust, jealousy, cowardice, anxiety, and apathy, to name just a few. But Jung recognized that the shadow holds more than just our faults and shortcomings.

The shadow can also be a storehouse of untapped gifts, talents, and concealed potentials. Parts of ourselves that are beautiful and powerful but somehow never got fully expressed make up the golden aspects of the shadow. This includes dormant creativity, confidence, integrity, as well as repressed positive emotions.

Jung believed that achieving psychological wholeness and inner peace requires reconciling our shadow. The persona—the social mask we wear—must come into harmony with the denied, hidden shadow side. Integrating these split-off pieces of ourselves allows us to become more complete, authentic, and self-aware.

This process of shadow integration was deemed essential by Jung for personal growth, enlightened relationships, and showing up fully in the world. Understanding our dark side brings self-acceptance, compassion, increased consciousness, and the ability to relate to others constructively. Leaving the shadow unknown and unexplored keeps us lost in patterns of ignorance, denial, and toxicity.

Defining Today's Shadow Self

While Jung introduced the seminal concept of the shadow over a century ago, how do modern thinkers define and describe this phenomenon? What does the shadow self look like in today's world?

Contemporary psychology upholds Jung's original notion of the shadow as the parts of ourselves we repress, disown or are not consciously aware of. Hidden weaknesses, fears, suppressed memories, trauma, antisocial desires, and unacceptable urges all fall under the shadow's domain.

But today we recognize the shadow is more than just a dumping ground for flaws and damages. Our shadow sides contain many positives—untapped talents, dormant potential, and unused strengths. Even seemingly negative attributes may have value if we understand them properly.

For example, repressed anger may just be assertiveness lost. Impulsiveness can also represent spontaneity. Selfishness could reflect a lost sense of boundaries and self-care. And anxiety may be signaling important inner truths we're afraid to confront.

Modern thinkers also emphasize the role culture and society play in shaping our shadows. The many "isms" that plague us—like racism, sexism, classism and ageism—exert enormous influence. Family dynamics, trauma, and collective wounds inherited from previous generations also contribute. We repress parts of ourselves that these forces judge as inferior, dangerous or unacceptable.

Overall, our shadows represent who we truly are beneath pretense and conditioning. The shadow self points to light as much as it points to darkness within us. Befriending and understanding this inner darkness is the key to living authentically and compassionately engaging the world around us.

The Collective Unconscious and Shadows

One of Carl Jung's most renowned theories was that of the "collective unconscious." This concept refers to a dimension of the unconscious mind that is universal and shared by all human beings across cultures, places, and times. Jung believed that this collective layer of the psyche exerts great influence on how our individual shadows take form.

Jung believed that the collective unconscious contains primordial, archetypal memories, patterns of behavior, and images that we inherit from our ancestors. These ancestral memories stretch back to the earliest origins of humankind. They are part of our psychic heritage as a species and include ideas such as gods, daemons, people, or processes that appear repeatedly in our history and culture as a species.

This universal psyche shapes each person's developing unconscious. As we grow up, the collective unconscious interacts with our personal experiences to construct the architecture of our inner world. Our unique life events get filtered through this generational lens, blending personal and collective shadows.

Jung suggested several ways the collective unconscious contributes in forming our individual shadow selves:

Archetypal Imagery - Certain symbolic figures reside in the collective unconscious that we all have access to - the Mother, the Father, the

Child, the Hero. These patterns help shape our perceptions, including how we identify undesirable traits to repress.

Inherited Behaviors - We carry instinctual, primal modes of being passed down genetically and energetically through countless generations. These influence how we construct our shadow sides.

Cultural Conditioning - The norms, values, and beliefs of our culture around gender, race, class, etc. contribute to the individual shadow's composition. Certain attributes become deemed 'light' or 'dark' based on societal programming.

Family Legacies - Unresolved traumas, toxic patterns, and suppressed emotions in our family tree trickle down subconsciously, concealing parts of ourselves deemed unacceptable by ancestors.

The Shadow of Humanity - Collective shadows around violence, domination, prejudice and environmental destruction permeate all our psyches, contributing to the personal shadows we form.

Here are some examples of how the collective unconscious may participate in developing our unique shadow selves:

1. Archetypal imagery around masculinity as aggressive and femininity as passive shapes gender shadows and development.

2. An inherited propensity towards hot-headedness makes anger something to suppress rather than skillfully transform.

3. Social taboos around sexuality cause desires, pleasures, and the body to become shadowed for many.

4. Generational addiction and abuse prompt repression of painful memories and undesirable impulses.

5. Colonial mentality dynamics condition certain races to ac-

tivate the shadow through racial projections.

6. Societal messages that selfishness and vulnerability equal weakness drive repression of self-care needs.

7. Toxic masculinity suppresses receptivity, caregiving, and emotional sensitivity in men.

8. Patriarchal conditioning teaches the feminine to disown ambition, strength, and power in herself.

As you can see, the collective unconscious powerfully influences the composition of our secret shadow selves across many dimensions, some of which we may even not be aware of. The cultural norms, family wounds, archetypal energies alive in humanity's psyche, and more all leave their imprint.

Jung believed making the unconscious conscious was key for unlocking greater self-awareness and wholeness. Part of this work involves illuminating how the collective psyche has uniquely shaped our individual shadows. When we shed light on this material, we can begin reclaiming and integrating the lost parts of ourselves.

For example, a man exploring his repressed feminine side (anima) recognizes how traditional masculine archetypes influenced suppressing these qualities. Or a woman unpacks how generational trauma caused her to adopt a false shadow persona of a 'good girl' to cover up authentic expressions of anger and strength.

In these ways, understanding the collective forces that molded our shadow delivers freedom and choice around how we wish to relate to these previously unconscious aspects moving forward. Our destiny is no longer constrained by the past. We reclaim our wholeness.

How Your Shadow Was Created

The seeds of our shadows first take root in childhood. We are born pure and unfiltered, expressing a full spectrum of human emotions and impulses without shame or limitation. But society quickly imposes categories of "good" and "bad", shaping us to fit in its box.

Through indirect cues and outright criticism, we learn which natural parts of ourselves are acceptable and which must be banished from view. Vulnerable and dependent on our caregivers, we contort ourselves to gain love and approval. Slowly, we split off the pieces deemed messy, ugly or wrong.

For instance, a highly sensitive child might be scolded for crying "over nothing" and "acting like a baby." They quickly learn it's safer to bottle up feelings than risk rejection for being too emotional. Over time, this suppressed aspect forms part of their shadow.

Gender roles also feed the shadow. Boys are often shamed for any behavior considered feminine or weak. Girls learn that assertiveness and anger make them unladylike. Qualities outside rigid stereotypes get cast into darkness. Well-meaning parents and teachers demand conformity in hopes of protecting us. But forced suppression of our true natures is deeply wounding. We adopt false selves adapted for survival, not fulfillment.

Beyond childhood, the shadow continues growing throughout life. Peer pressure in adolescence coerces us to alter or hide parts of ourselves to belong. At work, we obscure anything that contradicts our professional image. Standard roles leave little space for uniqueness. We learn that love and belonging require playing a part and obscuring anything that others may find strange, threatening or undesirable. Safety becomes equated with wearing a socially acceptable mask.

Even our own distorted thinking plays a role. The insecure ego clings to a rigid self-image. If being smart defines our identity, admitting confusion gets suppressed. If we pride ourselves on being self-reliant, needing others feels terrifyingly vulnerable. Internalizing society's standards, we police our own thoughts and emotions. Things that don't match our self-concept sneak into the shadows, however essential for wholeness. We betray our true selves for acceptance.

The cost of this denial is profound. Our shadows don't simply disappear once banished. They influence us covertly, manifesting through anxiety, emptiness, addictions and broken relationships. Healing requires bringing them into the light.

Our shadows speak to the uniqueness we learned to hide and the pain we learned to silence.

The Shadow-Self

Now that you understand a little about Carl Jung and his work, as well as the origins of our shadows, let's have a look at our Shadow-Self.

To put it briefly, in Jungian psychology, the shadow is either an unconscious feature of thepersonality that the conscious ego doesn't identify in itself or the whole ofthe unconscious. It's everything we're not fully aware of; the unknown, darkside of ourselves.

Since the shadow isinstinctive and irrational, it often projects onto others what we unconsciouslyview as faults within ourselves. Nobody likes to think badly of themselves sowe keep these parts of our personality hidden, believing it's "them" and not "us". But, the longer we ignore or deny this part of ourselves, the more we give it the power to create what we dislike or fear most.

This isn't a psychology book though since I'm focused in dealing with spiritual issues. I want to teach you how to recognize, understand, and finally make peace with your shadow-self. Does that mean you should destroy that part of yourself? Get rid of those dark parts that have caused youso much trouble and frustration? No.

Getting rid of your shadow would be like cutting yourself in half. You need both to have balanceand to be whole. We're merely going to shine light into those dark places soyou can see them more clearly rather than being blind to them. You'll make peace with these issues and learn to use them to your advantage. But, it won't happen overnight. Instead, it will be like peeling back layer after layer of anenormous onion.

When I refer to your dark side or shadow-self, I'm referring to the anger, fear, sadness, rejection,shame, denial, and embarrassment that we all stuff deep inside. Why do we do this? Because, we're taught from a young age that these feelings aren't acceptable, so we go through life pasting on a false front and adding more layers to the shadow within.

Whether you've struggled with money, weight, love, or just about anything else, you can bet that your shadow-self needs to be faced at long last and worked on. Once you do, you should notice your life changing in both small and dramatic ways. You'll attract more positive people and better opportunities. Life will be happier, smoother, and far more abundant.

In my years of practice, I've seen fellow practioners go from loveless or abusive relationships to stable, soulmate marriages. People who have declared bankruptcy and are on the verge of homelessness now having a steady paycheck and positive financial futures. Those who have gone from being severely overweight and riddled with pain, to reaching their goal weight and feeling healthier and more energetic than they had in decades.

I'll be honest though, shadow work isn't for the faint of heart or those who give up easily. After all, you're going to be facing some scary, negative, and unflattering things that have been buried inside you for some time. These deep-seated traits are usually formed in early childhood, and are then compounded on over time.

You can't deny the existence of your shadow any longer. I can guarantee that if you've been repeating the same patterns and attracting the same type of people and eventsin your life, no matter how hard you've tried to make changes, your shadow-self is the one in charge. Let's change all that. Let's get to work on creating the type of life you've always wanted!

The Ego vs the Shadow-Self

Our shadow self begins forming early in life as we absorb messages about what emotions and behaviors are acceptable or "good." Anything deemed inappropriate gets shoved into the darkness. Over time, we build elaborate layers of denial around these disowned aspects of ourselves.

The problem is, our shadow doesn't just disappear because we ignore it. In fact, it can take on a destructive life of its own, controlling our thoughts and actions in ways we don't intend. Jung called this the "dark side" of our psyche.

Have you ever self-sabotaged when on the verge of achieving a long-held goal? Or reacted intensely to someone exhibiting flaws you can't tolerate in yourself? Do you attract the same dysfunctional relationship dynamics over and over? Chances are your shadow self is running the show from backstage.

The only way to reclaim our power is to stop fighting these inner demons and bring them into the light of awareness. To acknowledge that we are all both light and dark. Our wholeness lies in embracing all that we are - not just the polished ego we present to the world.

Shining A Light on Our Inner Darkness

What exactly lurks in our personal shadow? It's unique for each of us, but some common shadows include:

- Raw emotions like anger, jealousy, grief, anxiety, sadness. Feelings our ego deems bad or unacceptable.

- Immoral or taboo desires that clash with our conscious values. Rage, lust, greed.

- Behaviors that contradict our outward persona. A competitive drive that opposes a nice, cooperative image.

- Traumatic memories our psyche tries to bury. Events that shaped our shadows.

- Core beliefs about ourselves that don't align with our ego identity. Feelings of inadequacy and fear.

- Parts of ourselves we judge harshly or deem flaws. The very qualities we can't abide in others.

- Owning and valuing these disowned parts is the only path to wholeness. But first, we have to shine a light into those inner recesses through radical self-reflection.

Some ways to illuminate your shadow side:

- Notice emotional reactions to others. What judgments or criticisms reflect aspects of yourself you deny?

- Keep a journal and record dreams. Uncover recurring themes and suppressed conflicts.

- List your strengths and weaknesses. Are there undervalued qualities you rejected long ago?

- Explore past experiences that may have shaped your shadows. Heal those inner wounds with compassion.

- Share your process with someone you trust. Speaking your shadows helps to release their power.

- Envision meeting your shadow. What does it look like? What is it trying to say about your hidden needs?

- Try Gestalt dialogue to externalize and integrate different aspects of your psyche.

Owning our shadow self takes courage, but allows us to finally embrace the totality of who we are.

Your Many Selves

Our minds create an image of who we think we are, shaped by our memories, lessons, and experiences from a young age. This self-image often lacks awareness of our true nature. As a result, we can feel trapped in cycles of frustration and confusion. We may dislike parts of ourselves because we've decided certain traits or characteristics are unacceptable.

It's important to understand that there's no single "right" way to be. In reality, we contain vast potential - we are capable of experiencing and interpreting life in countless ways. Our unconscious patterns and agendas operate automatically, like a robot. While this is helpful for basic bodily functions like breathing, it can be problematic for psychological issues. For example, we may continually try to heal old wounds or seek approval from our parents, even long after it's useful or relevant.

We all have different sides to our personality - the ideal version of ourselves, the face we show to others, and who we are in private moments. To find wholeness and reach our full potential, we need to accept all these aspects of ourselves, even those we've tried to ignore or push away. By acknowledging and integrating our various "selves," including the parts we consider flaws or weaknesses, we can become more complete and authentic individuals.

This process of self-acceptance and integration isn't always easy, but it's a crucial part of personal growth.

Who You Think You Are

We all have an idea in our minds of who we are - an identity formed over years of experiences, teachings, and memories. This self-image contains the traits and behaviors we find acceptable and want to uphold. It's our ego, our social mask - the version of ourselves we feel comfortable presenting to the world.

Our ego self craves consistency. We want to be seen as "good" by maintaining an image we've built up. So we cling to this limited construct, believing it reflects our true nature. But this curated identity can never encompass everything we are. There are endless other sides to ourselves that remain unseen.

Who You Think You Are Not

Anything that doesn't fit into our accepted self-concept gets relegated to our shadow - the parts of ourselves we don't like or want to acknowledge. Behaviors that seem inappropriate, qualities we judge as flaws, emotions we deem bad or unnecessary.

We feel averse to these disowned aspects of ourselves. When they arise, we experience discomfort, negativity, and contraction. We criticize ourselves for not living up to our ego ideal. The shadow seems to threaten our sense of self, so we pretend it doesn't exist.

But in reality, we have the capacity to be anything, not just the limited way we define ourselves. We are ever-changing and multi-dimensional. By clinging to a rigid identity, we lock ourselves into repetitive thought patterns and behaviors. We resist growth, afraid to step outside the lines we've drawn.

Who Are You Really?

No one can define for certain the entirety of another's being. We are far more than any label, story, or image. Our essential nature lies beyond the mind's ability to conceptualize.

Pure awareness - consciousness observing itself - is closer to our real self than any constructed identity. When we release attachment to being any one way, we open to the flow of life and all its possibilities. We connect more deeply with the formless, timeless essence at our core.

By fixating on our ego, we fragment the wholeness of who we are. But if we embrace each moment with fresh eyes, without preconceived judgments, we can experience life more fully.

Why Things Run Unconsciously

We often operate on autopilot, with ingrained mental and emotional patterns running the show. Thoughts and behaviors become unconscious through repetition over time. Traumatic or unresolved experiences also sink into our unconscious realm.

The mind craves efficiency, so it automates processes we repeat frequently. But this can obstruct awareness. We fail to recognize unhealthy or self-defeating patterns rooted in past events or conditioning.

By cultivating presence through practices like meditation, we illuminate the darkness of our unconscious mind. More moments become available to conscious choice, free from the inertia of past habits. We gain power to reshape our inner world.

What This Has to Do with Shadow Work

Shadow work involves uncovering repressed aspects of ourselves that our egos dismiss or deny. All those intense emotions, buried memories, and undesirable traits that lurk beneath the surface.

By exploring our personal darkness with radical self-honesty and compassion, we can finally integrate and own all of who we are. We stop projecting unwanted qualities onto others. We align our actions with our truth.

This deeply personal work requires courage and perseverance. But embracing our shadow liberates us from inner fragmentation and conflict. We release limiting definitions of self that hold us back. We discover the potential to live and lead from a place of wholeness and authenticity.

When we make peace with the entirety of who we are, we can relate to ourselves and others from a place of wholeness and compassion. Our unconscious patterns no longer control our thoughts and behaviors. We finally become the authors of our own experience, creative and conscious participants in this adventure called life.

Your Shadow Is Real

The shadow is not some abstract concept or benign theory. This hidden part of ourselves is an ever-present, living reality that profoundly shapes our inner and outer worlds. By better understanding this subconscious realm, we can untangle ourselves from its grip and step into greater self-awareness.

What Is the Shadow Exactly? It represents the accumulation of all thoughts, emotions, urges, and aspects of ourselves that we deem unacceptable. It's a storage bin for anything that contradicts the limited identity our egos cling to.

This unclaimed baggage starts forming early in life as we learn to edit ourselves to gain love, approval and belonging. Young children express the full range of human experience without filters. But over time, we're taught to reshape ourselves by inhibiting certain feelings and behaviors deemed "bad." Anything we disown out of shame, guilt or judgment gets locked away in the shadow's darkness. It doesn't disappear - it lives on beneath our conscious awareness. This buried vault contains both so-called negative emotions like anger, jealousy and hurt, as well as positive ones like joy, passion and excitement.

By young adulthood, after years of burying parts of ourselves, our shadows hold tremendous stores of unseen thoughts, needs and impulses. Like a second self, this raw, unfiltered material continues to influence us, though we pretend it doesn't exist.

How Our Shadow Manifests

The shadow finds covert ways to make itself known by directing our behaviors, choices and perceptions. For instance:

- We may act out in anger over minor frustrations because suppressed rage stored deep within needs release.

- We criticise others harshly for qualities that mirror our own rejected flaws and faults.

- Addictions provide escape from pent-up emotions we don't know how to handle.

- By staying small and playing it safe, we avoid risking failure, protecting egos too fragile to bear much light.

The shadow also attracts people and situations that force us to face our hidden issues. The boss who triggers our deepest insecurities acts as a mirror, reflecting back wounds we've denied. The partner who reopens childhood trauma offers a chance for healing if we have the courage to see it.

Like a splinter in our psyche, the shadow continually pricks and pains us until we work to remove it. Rather than attacking or rejecting this inner darkness, we must embrace it with radical compassion.

Side Effects Of Our Shadow

The shadow is the home of our disowned thoughts, feelings and impulses. Whatever aspects of ourselves we deem unacceptable get relegated to this inner darkness. But exiling parts of our being comes at a steep price, as the shadow continues shaping our lives in unseen ways.

When we pretend our shadows don't exist, we remain fractured, blocked off from our deepest truths. The consequences of this denial permeate all aspects of life. Here are some common side effects of leaving our shadows unaddressed:

1. Relationship Struggles

Our intimate partnerships often suffer most from our ignored shadows. We attract partners who allow us to reenact old painful patterns from childhood. We recreate unhealthy dynamics from the past in hopes of finally resolving them.

For instance, if one had a controlling parent, one may repeatedly attract or be attracted to controlling romantic partners. On the surface this seems baffling. But on a subconscious level, stepping back into this familiar role offers a chance for healing by changing the way we respond.

Yet most remain unaware of what their shadows seek to resolve. So they find themselves on the same hurtful merry-go-round again and again. Friendships and family bonds also become strained as our shadows project themselves onto those close to us.

2. Feeling Like an Outsider

With much of our true selves buried in the shadows, we end up feeling disconnected - from others and ourselves. We long for intimacy and belonging, but walls around our hearts prevent true closeness.

Our unresolved pain makes us feel fundamentally flawed. Unworthy of the love, understanding and support we crave. We isolate further in unconscious efforts to hide our shameful shadows from view. But this only breeds more loneliness.

3. Repeating Destructive Patterns

Until we do our inner work, the shadow drives us to repeat self-defeating behaviors. We find ourselves stuck in jobs that drain us. Addictions that offer only temporary relief. Financial crises that arise just as prosperity feels within reach.

The shadow manifests through these stuck cycles that thwart our dreams. What we repress internally gets projected externally. We must address the root causes rather than just the symptoms.

4. Destructive Reactive Behaviors

Nice as we aim to be, unresolved anger, hurt and fear still erupt from our shadows when certain triggers arise. We act out in ways that contradict our values and ideals of who we want to be.

Lashing out at loved ones in anger or numbingly scrolling for hours serve as pressure valves for what we won't acknowledge inside. But expressing our shadows destructively only strengthens their influence.

5. Low Motivation and Energy

Carrying around heavy shadows drains our life force. We lack passion and curiosity for life. Feel weighed down by invisible burdens. The light inside dims.

Rather than setting goals and taking steps to achieve them, we just distract ourselves from a vague sense of frustration and discontent. We float along doing the minimum, never fully showing up. But this apathy keeps us playing small in lives that feel dull and drained of color.

All these symptoms stem from the same chronic disconnection from our wholeness. But we need not suffer the shadow's effects forever. By courageously exploring its wisdom with compassion, we can reclaim and integrate our lost pieces.

Here are some steps to mitigate the shadow's unhealthy influence:

- Notice repetitive destructive patterns playing out. Ask what the underlying cause might be.

- Make a daily practice of emotional check-ins. Don't reject difficult feelings.

- Unearth repressed memories, interests and fantasies. See what clues they hold.

- Examine your criticisms and irritations about others. Look for mirrors.

- Own and express your full humanity - including all the so-called flaws.

- Share your shadow exploration with trusted allies who offer non-judgmental reflections.

- Respond to darkness with caring curiosity, not fear or denial. Ask what it needs from you.

Owning our shadows relieves us from endlessly wrestling with ourselves. We attract healthier relationships, act from integrity, and feel energized by our purpose. No longer divided inside, we step into lives of passion, meaning and joy.

Why Befriending Our Shadow is Essential

It's tempting to view the shadow as an enemy - an unruly beast trying to undermine our quest for health and happiness. But shaming or demonizing parts of ourselves only strengthens their hold.

Integrating our shadows is the only path to inner peace. This requires moving beyond the ego's simplistic categories of good/bad, right/wrong, positive/negative. Holding our suppressed emotions and impulses in the light of honest awareness diffuses their destructive power over us.

Owning the full spectrum of our humanity allows us to act from authenticity instead of inner conflict. We can pursue dreams we deem unacceptably bold. Feel everything deeply without shame or judgment. Speak and stand in our truths.

Befriending our shadows frees us from endlessly trying to hide our flaws and avoid pain. We develop the courage to be fully ourselves, messy humanness and all.

Practical Steps to Shadow Integration:

- Notice repetitive negative patterns playing out in your life. What might they reveal about buried emotions or impulses?

- Explore your triggers. What provokes disproportionate reactions? These sensitivities likely connect to shadow material.

- Uncover projections. The traits that irritate you in others often reflect disowned aspects of yourself.

- Examine your fantasies. These reveal hidden longings and offer clues to under-developed aspects seeking growth.

- Dig into memories you avoid revisiting. Our shadows house old wounds that need airing.

- View nightmares and scary dreams as messages from the shadow trying to get your attention.

- Active imagination exercises can help build a dialogue with your shadow. Don't judge what arises.

- Share your shadow exploration with trusted allies. Their feedback helps shed light on your blind spots.

- Move toward, not away from, strong emotions that feel uncomfortable or confusing.

- Respond to your shadow with curiosity and compassion, not more repression. What does it need?

Owning our shadows liberates powerful energies once trapped fighting inward. Once embraced, our shadows become partners invested in our growth, not adversaries. With courage, we can reclaim and integrate all the lost parts of ourselves into a coherent whole. We shed limiting masks and stand fully revealed at last.

The Impact of the Shadow on Daily Life

As you would understand by now, we all have shadows; they begin forming in childhood as we're taught to edit, inhibit and reshape ourselves to gain love and approval. Anything considered "bad" or unacceptable gets shoved into the shadow realm. Over time, we construct elaborate masks to hide our messy humanness. We lock up anything too emotional, too honest or too real that might crack the facade. But these disowned aspects don't just disappear. They influence us covertly, manifesting in unexpected and destructive ways. They drive our behaviors, choices, relationships and habits in ways we can't fully see or understand.

Unconscious behaviors rooted in the shadow can sabotage relationships, derail careers and undermine health. Have you ever lashed out in anger only to later wonder "where did that come from?" Do you self-sabotage when success seems within reach? Does anxiety arise in situations that "shouldn't" make you nervous? The shadow is likely at play and until we shine a light on these inner shadows, we remain fragmented and at war within ourselves.

Repressed memories and emotions buried deep within escape through the cracks of our awareness. They drive compulsive habits, irrational fears, chronic dissatisfaction and other patterns that we may seem to repeat in our lives knowingly or unknowingly. Simply put, our shadow controls our thoughts and behaviors; we often fail to recognize its influence because we're wearing masks even to ourselves. Shining a light on our inner darkness is the only path to freedom.

The shadow reveals itself in our lives in subtle and not-so-subtle ways. Though we construct elaborate masks to hide the messy, imperfect parts of ourselves, our repressed feelings and impulses don't just disappear. They continue influencing our behaviors, choices and perceptions below the level of conscious awareness.

Our Shadow and Bad Choices

We've all made decisions we later regretted - choices that seemed to defy logic and work against our best interests. In hindsight, we scratch our heads wondering, "What was I thinking?" More often than not, these puzzling lapses in judgment can be traced back to the shadow.

When this buried part of ourselves gets triggered, it hijacks our decision-making faculties and leads us astray. But rather than beating ourselves up over shadow-driven choices, we can mine them for insight.

First, it's important to understand the shadow represents our disowned thoughts, feelings and impulses. It contains raw, unfiltered emotions and instincts from childhood onward that our egos deemed messy or unacceptable.

We lock this unruly, immature material away to present a polished social mask. But the shadow still influences us in unseen ways. When unleashed, it overrides logic with knee-jerk reactions and temporary relief-seeking.

For instance, say you just emerged from an abusive relationship. The breakup leaves you feeling unstable and unable to think clearly. In this vulnerable state, your shadow may convince you to toss aside rational considerations and spontaneously move across the country to escape the pain.

Like a defiant child, the shadow acts on impulse, wanting what it wants when it wants it. It operates on the logic of a 5-year-old or 15-year-old you - not the mature adult you've become. When handed the reins in times of stress, it predictably steers us wrong.

As frustrating as shadow-driven choices are, they provide opportunities to unburden ourselves of old baggage. Running from problems keeps painful patterns alive. But facing the realities these choices bring can free us at last.

For instance, while moving cross-country on a whim may initially seem liberating, reality soon sinks in. Without your support system nearby, and the practical challenges of establishing a new life, loneliness and hardship follow.

Rather than judging yourself, summon self-compassion. Then look for the gift in this unwise choice. Perhaps it forces you to confront childhood trauma you've avoided. Or build resilience and problem-solving skills you lack.

By learning from our shadow-driven choices, we can start making decisions from a place of wholeness. We develop awareness of when this wounded inner self tries to sabotage our growth. Our shadow becomes an ally rather than adversary - guiding us towards the light instead of into the same old traps.

Our Shadow in Personal Relationships

Our shadow selves inevitably affect the way we relate to romantic partners, friends, family, and colleagues. Common problematic manifestations include:

- *Projection* - When we can't accept certain feelings or impulses within, we attribute them to others and react accordingly. For example, someone who won't admit their own anger may constantly perceive others as aggressive.

- *Displacement* - Repressed emotions get redirected onto safer targets. We snap at a partner when we're actually upset about work. Our shadow finds a substitute.

- *Victim mentality* - By disowning our power, we view ourselves as helpless victims of others' behavior. But playing the victim prevents us from taking responsibility for our role.

- *Control issues* - Trying to control people and situations often stems from our own inner lack of control. We seek to regulate external factors to avoid facing our shadows.

- *Addictions* - Addictive behaviors can originate from an unconscious urge to avoid, distract from or medicate inner pain. But they prevent shadow integration.

Owning our shadows is the only way to stop projecting them onto relationships. For example, acknowledging one's own jealousy allows us to perceive a partner more clearly, minus the distorting lens of projection. We regain power over our inner world.

Through courageous shadow work, we can become more authentic partners and friends. We express ourselves from a place of wholeness. Our words and actions align with our truths, rather than being driven by unconscious patterns.

Our Shadow's Influence on Decision-Making

Our shadow selves don't disappear just because we try to ignore them. In fact, they often secretly steer our decision-making, leading to choices that contradict our stated values and goals. Here's how:

- *Unconscious emotional drives* - Suppressed feelings like anger, hurt, or envy can compel decisions meant to soothe those wounds, not serve our highest good. We may choose a partner who echoes a toxic dynamic from childhood in an attempt to finally resolve it.

- *Hidden desires* - Cravings and passions we consider "negative" remain alive in our shadows, where they drive compulsive behavior. An affair that jeopardizes a marriage may be driven by this repressed desire.

- *Fear-based choices* - Anxiety stemming from our shadow's fears can lead to playing it safe but feeling restless and unfulfilled. We might stay in a dead-end job rather than pursuing our dreams.

- *Contrarian tendencies* - Making decisions that subconsciously rebel against our conscious values reflects an inner conflict between ego ideals and shadow desires. It stems from a fractured psyche.

- *Escapism* - Abusing substances, pursuing adrenaline highs, or compulsive habits offer escape from inner pain. But these shadow-fueled choices only lead us further astray.

Owning the parts of ourselves that scare or disturb us diffuses their control over our choices.

Our Shadow's Role in Workplace Dynamics

Our shadow selves don't clock out when we go to work. Unresolved inner conflicts and suppressed emotions inevitably surface in our professional lives, often in counterproductive ways:

- *Defensiveness* - Constructive feedback or criticism may pierce our thinly-veiled egos, provoking a surge of denial or defensiveness from our shadows. We feel attacked when the issue is really our own lack of self-worth.

- *Power struggles* - Competing for dominance in unconscious efforts to shore up fragile egos is a common manifestation. We may resist colleague's ideas to assert our superiority.

- *Sabotage* - Self-defeating habits like chronic lateness, disorganization or self-medication provide short-term relief but reflect and reinforce inner turmoil. The shadow undermines our success.

- *Projection* - Seeing negative traits in co-workers that we can't accept in ourselves poisons relationships. The hyper-critical boss perceives laziness all around her, blind to that tendency in herself.

- *Resistance* - Chafing under authority often signals an inner conflict with power. We may project negative traits like tyranny or incompetence onto bosses we subconsciously view as threatening.

Doing our inner shadow work allows us to act from wholeness, not fear or ego, at work. We take responsibility for our role in conflicts. Feedback is illuminating, not threatening. We become more authentic colleagues and leaders.

Owning our weaknesses and darker impulses diminishes their control over us. We accept constructive criticism with grace and maturity. We collaborate generously instead of competing to overcome inner doubts. Integrating all aspects of ourselves leads to more harmony and fulfillment in our professional lives.

Examples of The Shadow

To better understand how the shadow operates, let's explore some hypothetical, yet highly relatable, examples. These scenarios illustrate how unacknowledged inner conflicts can manifest through our external lives, often in ways that seem confusing or self-defeating.

As these examples below show, our shadow finds ways to color our reality, interact with our egos, and make itself known. Until we bring it into the light of awareness with compassion, we remain divided against ourselves, pulled in different directions by competing impulses and beliefs.

Example 1:

Meet Sarah, a dedicated accountant at a thriving tech startup. To her colleagues, Sarah is clever, diligent and highly competent. She arrives early, leaves late, and consistently meets every deadline. Sarah's technical skills and strong work ethic have earned her recognition and promotions over her 5 years at the company.

By all outward measures, Sarah is an invaluable asset driving the finance department. But inwardly, she feels anything but valued. A sense of inadequacy and self-doubt plagues her. Despite tangible evidence that her contributions matter, she can't internalize it.

During team meetings, Sarah shrinks from sharing ideas. She assumes her perspective isn't worthwhile or unique. When her manager praises her performance, she shrugs it off as just being polite. Constructive feedback cuts especially deep, affirming her belief that she just doesn't measure up.

Sarah recalls being an insecure child, struggling to believe in her own worth. As the middle of three highly intelligent sisters, she often felt unseen, her accomplishments overshadowed. Never quite pretty or smart enough in her own eyes. These painful memories lodged deep within Sarah's shadow.

Though she constructed a veneer of confidence as an adult, hints of those old wounds continued driving her behaviors. Sarah's shadow whispered that she didn't really deserve to be here. That someone better qualified would surely replace her soon enough.

So Sarah perseverated on perceived mistakes and shortcomings. She minimized praise, while criticism reinforced her inner narrative of inadequacy. Overpreparing for presentations then downplaying her expertise kept vulnerability at bay. But it also prevented Sarah from revealing her true talents.

This inner critic drove Sarah to overcompensate through tireless work, as if productivity could compensate for some inherent flaw only she could see. Long hours provided a distraction from deeper feelings of fraudulence. But striving and straining to prove herself was endless and exhausting.

Example 2:

Meet Michael, a successful corporate attorney who prides himself on being logical, responsible and always in control. He enjoys the image others have of him as a pragmatic and highly competent professional. But beneath the polished surface lurks an unacknowledged shadow self longing for more spontaneity and adventure.

Michael maintains a structured routine of early mornings at the gym before heading to the office. His Tuesdays are spent on household chores and paying bills. Dinners out with his wife feel comforting and familiar. Weekends are mostly spent relaxing at home.

This orderly lifestyle provides Michael with a sense of stability. He values the predictability that combats the chaos of his high-pressure job. But occasionally, an urge arises to step outside the lines he has so carefully drawn. A restlessness surfaces, though Michael quickly suppresses it, deeming such impulses irresponsible or indulgent.

But the needs of Michael's shadow find other ways to manifest. Once in a while, he accepts a last-minute invitation for a night out with colleagues, despite an early morning obligation. He finds himself buying concert tickets on impulse rather than saving for a rainy day as usual.

Michael also notices himself enthralled by accounts of people pursuing exotic adventures and bold life changes. He quickly explains away this passing interest, yet finds himself drawn in again and again. Through this, his shadow signals unmet needs for more passion and spontaneity.

In rare unguarded moments, Michael's inner wild child takes over. He books a sudden weekend getaway, or makes a risky purchase. While part of Michael feels exhilarated, he also feels guilty and anxious afterwards about acting out of character. He reproaches himself for this perceived loss of self-discipline.

But Michael has nothing to feel ashamed about. With compassionate awareness, he can acknowledge this vibrant part of himself seeking expression. Rather than rejecting his shadow, he can explore integrating just a touch of playfulness and adventure into his lifestyle.

In our first example, Sarah, an accomplished employee constantly feels undervalued at work, despite tangible achievements and praise. Her shadow harbors a deep sense of unworthiness rooted in childhood experience. Though repressed, this belief taints her self-perception. She filters feedback through a lens of inadequacy, diminishing signs of success that contradict her inner critic. What remains unconscious controls her.

With the right support and awareness, Sarah can finally acknowledge the shadow beliefs eroding her self-confidence. Rather than harshly repressing her feelings of unworthiness and insecurity, she can hold them with gentle compassion. This emotional integration quiets her inner critic's endless judgments. Owning and honoring every part of herself allows Sarah to act from a place of wholeness. She can view feedback objectively, without projecting shameful meanings.

In the second example, Michael, a person who prides themselves on self-control has an unrecognized shadow craving spontaneity and adventure. This suppressed inner wild child might then manifest through impulsive behavior that disrupts their orderly world. However out of character, these actions provide cathartic release of the shadow's stifled needs.

Through small steps outside his comfort zone, Michael can meet his shadow's needs while staying true to his core values. He might plan a vacation doing something active like hiking or surfing. Or explore local events that spark that sense of novelty he craves. Owning and honoring his shadow will free Michael from inner conflict. He would no longer needs to swing between rigid self-control and erratic reckless release. Michael discovers he can mindfully include a taste of freedom and excitement within his responsible reality. More than a source of struggle, his shadow can become a teacher instead of a source of shame.

As these examples show, our shadow finds ways to color our reality, interact with our egos, and make itself known. Until we bring it into the light of awareness with compassion, we remain divided against ourselves, pulled in different directions by competing impulses and beliefs.

By acknowledging and working with our shadow, we can bring these unconscious influences into the light, allowing us to understand and integrate them. This integration leads to a more authentic and balanced life, where our decisions and relationships are more congruent with our true selves. It enables us to respond to life's challenges with greater awareness and emotional intelligence.

Identify Your Own Shadow

Have you ever met someone who immediately rubbed you the wrong way? Maybe they were rude, arrogant, lazy, or exhibited some other trait that you just couldn't stand. If so, that annoying person was likely a reflection of your own inner shadow.

According to the influential psychologist Carl Jung, the shadow represents aspects of ourselves that we repress, deny, or otherwise reject from our conscious identity. These disowned parts don't just disappear though. Instead, they continue to exist in our unconscious minds, often exerting their influence without us even realizing it.

One way our shadows show up is through a process called projection (more on this in a later chapter). When we come across qualities in others that we've disowned in ourselves, we "project" those traits onto those people, judging them harshly while remaining oblivious to the fact that they mirror parts of our own psyches. As Jung famously stated, "Everything that irritates us about others can lead us to an understanding of ourselves."

Have you ever judged someone as rude or obnoxious only to later realize you were irritable or curt yourself in that moment? Or condemned a person as arrogant when you were likewise overconfident about your own opinions? When we project our shadows in this way, we often end up disliking or looking down on others for the very flaws and faults we refuse to acknowledge in ourselves.

The key is to notice when these strong reactions get triggered. If someone really bothers you, makes you exceptionally angry or superior-feeling, that's a clue your shadow has entered the chat. The judgments you make about that person offer hints as to what disowned traits you may be projecting out.

For instance, say you instantly disliked a new co-worker who seemed loud and attention-seeking. You wrote them off as an obnoxious showboat without getting to know them. In that case, reflecting on times when you've also behaved in similarly grandiose or melodramatic ways could reveal disowned aspects of your own shadow at play.

Or imagine you meet someone you consider a complete airhead. You feel intellectually superior and assume they must be dumb as rocks. Well, perhaps there are areas where you've denied your own ignorance or lack of knowledge. Owning that part of your shadow could dampen those feelings of arrogant condescension.

Now, don't get me wrong. Sometimes people actually are just rude, arrogant, annoying, or inappropriate! This isn't about pretense or denial. However, when you have an intensely negative reaction, when someone really "gets under your skin" or makes you feel you're much "better than" them, that's a red flag your shadow may be running the show.

It takes courage to honestly investigate those vulnerable parts of ourselves. But embracing our shadows is how we integrate our whole selves and stop unwittingly projecting unwanted traits onto others. We all contain endless facets - both "light" and "dark." The psyche is not static, but rather a spectrum of potentials that emerge in different contexts.

Consider times when you felt jealousy, rage, shame, insecurity, or apathy. Perhaps you experienced greed, manipulation, selfishness, or a lack of empathy. In certain situations, you likely have the capacity to exhibit any human behavior, both admirable and ugly. We all do. But when we deny or compartmentalize those unsavory parts, they don't disappear. They lurk beneath the surface, outside our conscious awareness.

By radically accepting the entirety of who we are - not just selectively identifying with positive traits like kindness or intelligence - we can recognize when our unresolved shadows get externally projected. We still want to cultivate our highest selves, of course! But acknowledging our complete humanity helps us become more compassionate and less reactive. We relate to others and ourselves with more wisdom and wholeness.

So next time someone rubs you the wrong way, pause and ask yourself what uncomfortable trait gets triggered in their presence. What judgmental labels do you attach? Then explore within. See if you can find even the faint glimmer of that quality inside yourself. There's no need for shame or guilt - just acceptance and ownership.

Uncovering Your Hidden Shadow

The shadow represents repressed aspects of ourselves that our egos reject. These disowned qualities don't disappear, however. They lurk beneath the surface, outside conscious awareness. When triggered, they tend to get projected onto others. Those strong negative reactions provide clues to unraveling our shadows.

For instance, say you meet someone and instantly peg them as arrogant. You have a visceral aversion to their boastful, self-important manner. In that scenario, your intense irritation likely reflects disowned egotistical or narcissistic traits in your own psyche. Perhaps you strive for humility, yet suppress any grandiose impulses under the surface. This denied arrogance then gets projected outward when you encounter it blatantly in someone else.

Or imagine you have an especially hard time respecting a flaky, disorganized colleague. You judge them as scattered and irresponsible. Well, your intense annoyance may signal disowned aspects of yourself that can also occasionally be unreliable or distractible. Disliking this quality in another makes it easier to deny in yourself.

The key is noticing when your emotions are strongly triggered. If someone provokes anger, irritation, resentment, or feelings of superiority, that's essentially your shadow material projecting onto them. The specific judgment or criticism you have about the person offers insight into what you may be denying within.

For example, say you consider a peer weak or cowardly because they avoid confrontation. However, reflecting honestly, there may have been times when you also shrunk back from difficult dialogues. Seeing this quality intensely in another can help you recognize those buried parts of yourself you've deemed undesirable or shameful.

Perhaps you are highly disgusted by a colleague's deceitfulness. You view them as totally immoral and lacking ethics. But probing deeper, can you find even small past instances where you were also less than completely honest in order to gain some advantage? Even this tiny human experience of fraudulence gets ferociously rejected from your self-image and ends up projected onto your unsuspecting coworker.

Again, sometimes people truly exhibit annoying or distasteful behaviors! This isn't about pretending everything is perfect or equally your responsibility. It's about learning to recognize unconscious dynamics that can get theatrically played out through our interactions with others.

Your shadow material will emerge in your reactions to people who rub you the wrong way. Pay close attention when you feel intense irritation, judgment, or feelings of superiority around someone. Chances are, what bothers you most about them is linked to disowned aspects of yourself.

What If Others Actually Are That Flawed?

It's true, sometimes people genuinely do exhibit the negative traits you find so grating. You're not always just projecting your shadow onto them. But even when flaws are real, your intense reaction still provides insight.

For example, say your boss truly is an incompetent micromanager. Their leadership style may legitimately be hindering your team's performance and work culture. In that case, your judgments aren't imagined projections. However, if you absolutely despise this boss with fiery contempt, that reveals something about you.

Perhaps you struggle with your own controlling tendencies and this trait gets fiercely rejected from your self-image. Witnessing it so blatantly in a superior activates those unresolved shadows, provoking volatile emotions.

Or imagine a colleague spreads nasty gossip and you condemn them as mean-spirited and malicious. Well, those behaviors may indeed be poor conduct. But if you become sanctimonious and view yourself as a paragon of virtue, you're likely disowning petty or vindictive impulses that all humans harbor to some degree. Your colleague's gossip simply provides a convenient hook upon which to hang disliked parts of yourself you fail to acknowledge.

Again, this isn't about feigning perfection or pretending no one possesses genuinely annoying flaws. Some people truly are gratingly flawed, unethical, or destructive. But when you have an intensely emotional reaction, that's the clue. The degree of your contempt, rage, or feeling of superiority reveals hidden, disowned aspects of your own shadow coming to the surface.

An integrated psyche that cultivates self-awareness reacts with wisdom and discernment, not blind hatred. For example, say a colleague deceives people at work for their own gain. Now, you may accurately assess this as unethical and criticize the behavior. But shouting that they're a worthless, evil liar who you now despise reflects poorly on your own character, not just theirs. Such extreme demonizing reveals your shadow material, not higher moral sense.

Or imagine you view an acquaintance as pitiful and weak for not standing up to their abusive partner. Your evaluation may contain truth. However, if you feel disgust and contempt for this person rather than empathy, that exposes your shadows around vulnerability or prioritizing self-worth. Your judgmental reaction only highlights your own disowned wounds and self-rejection.

The goal is to notice the difference between discernment and shadow-fueled contempt. Spot those moments when your emotions flare up and you absolutely detest or look down on another person. Ask what repressed traits get triggered in you. Then you can see past the projections to assess the real issues in a measured, compassionate way.

Over time, embracing the entirety of who we are diminishes reactive judgments. We still identify poor conduct when we see it. But by owning our shadows, we refrain from eviscerating people who activate those unconscious, disowned parts of ourselves.

Why We Lock Away Our Shadow

Even though our shadows represent natural aspects of being human, we often reject these traits and lock them in the unconscious. But why? For starters, we are wired for survival. Our egos want to keep us safe by presenting a likable image to others. Expressing socially unacceptable emotions like anger or insecurity threatens this goal. We worry that if people see our flaws and brokenness, we'll face rejection. And since we depend on our tribe for survival, banishment can feel life-threatening on a primal level.

This instinct starts in childhood. If we throw a tantrum or act selfishly and get scolded, we learn to bottle up the "unacceptable" parts of ourselves. We start hiding certain feelings in order to gain our parents' love and acceptance. Without even realizing it, we construct a facade of only our positive traits - denying the other side of our humanity.

Society also conditions us to filter away undesirable qualities. We absorb messages that things like failure, neediness, depression, greed, and vulnerability are abnormal or inappropriate. So we exile anything that contradicts our idealized mask in order to fit in and be considered "normal." Keeping our shadows hidden becomes essential for being embraced by our communities.

The result is we all end up wearing masks, showing only bright, polished parts of ourselves while keeping our messes neatly tucked away. It's enormously relieving when those socially scorned traits get projected onto others instead of being spotted in ourselves. And yet, rejecting half of who we are comes at a great cost.

For one, it's exhausting to constantly monitor and filter our true emotions to keep up appearances. We become unable to relax into our authentic selves, always worried about slipping up. It also disconnects us from others. The relationships we form remain superficial, since no one can get close without seeing our real, unfiltered humanity.

Most importantly, denying our shadows cuts us off from our inner wholeness. We ossify into rigid identities built on illusions. Seeing ourselves as solely gentle, strong, pious, or professional keeps us fragmented and limited. But just like yin needs yang - light needs dark. Integrating our flaws and fragility is what makes us complete.

So while it's tempting to keep ugly parts locked away where no one can see, this strategy is ultimately isolating and inauthentic.

Shadow Work and Self-Esteem

Our self-esteem is deeply influenced by our relationship with our inner shadow. After all, self-esteem is really about self-acceptance - and it's hard to fully accept ourselves when we're rejecting parts of who we are. Shadow work helps illuminate the roots of low self-esteem so we can cultivate true, holistic self-love.

From a young age, we learn to construct a certain self-image based on what's acceptable and unacceptable to show. This starts with our parents, but also gets shaped by friends, school, society, and culture. There are certain behaviors and traits we're conditioned to express, while others get banished into our subconscious shadows.

For example, maybe a young boy learns it's okay to express anger but not vulnerability. A young girl might be encouraged to be polite and quiet, but not loud and assertive. We quickly figure out what earns approval vs. judgment and shape our self-concept accordingly.

The parts we have to hide don't actually disappear though - they live on in our shadow. These disowned aspects of ourselves have nowhere to go, so our ego covers them up to maintain the familiar self-image. This split between "acceptable me" and "unacceptable me" lays the foundation for low self-worth.

Here's why: When we can only accept certain facets of ourselves, it means we're conditional with self-love. We end up constantly judging ourselves for perceived flaws and trying to live up to unrealistic ideals. Our shadow holds a well of unacknowledged talents, needs, and feelings that could help balance us out.

I remember always feeling like I had to be smart, helpful, and polite as a kid. My family didn't approve of emotional outbursts, impatience, or selfishness. So whenever those feelings arose, I'd feel ashamed and try to hide them. This caused a lot of anxiety and inner turmoil.

It wasn't until I started compassionately accepting those shadow aspects through my healing work that I found more self-acceptance. I realized my "darker" emotions gave me important information about my needs. My outward personality was out of balance and I was missing crucial parts of myself.

Owning our shadow allows us to be more whole. We can't practice true, unconditional self-love while rejecting core pieces of who we are. When we acknowledge our multidimensionality, we no longer rely on a rigid, artificial self-image for esteem.

Ultimately, shadow work dismantles the faulty dichotomy between "good me" vs "bad me." It helps us stop anxiously policing ourselves to meet expectations. We discover an expansive sense of identity beyond limiting social conditioning. When you no longer reject inner darkness, self-love becomes a given - not something you have to earn. True self-esteem flowers from embracing the light and shadow within each of us.

The Problem of Good vs Bad

A core reason many of us struggle with low self-esteem is that we split ourselves into "good" and "bad" parts. We construct an image of ourselves containing only socially acceptable, desirable traits. Anything we perceive as negative or shameful gets banished into our unconscious shadows.

This starts in childhood as we quickly learn which behaviors and emotions earn us attention and affection vs judgment or punishment. To feel loved and secure, we emphasize the "good me" our caregivers approve of. The "bad me" gets stuffed down out of awareness.

But those disowned aspects don't actually disappear. They remain present beneath our conscious personality, unconsciously influencing our thoughts and actions. Whenever they pop up, we judge ourselves harshly. We failed at suppressing the "bad" parts of us. This inner turmoil severely damages our self-esteem.

The key to building real self-confidence is accepting that all those supposedly negative traits are actually valid parts of our complex humanity. Every human has emotional triggers, selfish impulses, moments of weakness. It's the natural spectrum of being an imperfectly perfect human.

I used to be ashamed of my impatience, vanity, jealousy and other "flaws." Only when I embraced them with self-compassion did I stop anxiously trying to hide them. I realized I was whole all along, not just the polished image I portrayed.

When we stop dividing ourselves into good and bad, our self-judgment lifts. We no longer have to criticize ourselves every time a shadow aspect emerges. We understand we can be caring and also frustrated, humble and also proud, gentle and also angry. Our self-love becomes unconditional.

The Paradox of Self-Esteem

Many of us believe we need to do something to raise our self-esteem. We try to pump ourselves up with positive thinking or achieve certain goals. We attempt to suppress the parts of ourselves we don't like. But these strategies only offer fleeting confidence boosts. They don't address the paradox at the heart of authentic self-esteem.

What is this paradox? It's the fact that we already are inherently worthy and lovable as we are - but we feel we have to prove it or change ourselves first. We think some external change will finally help us accept ourselves, not realizing self-acceptance starts from within.

When we rely on external things to feel good enough, we make our esteem conditional. It becomes dependent on someone else's validation, looking or acting a certain way, hitting milestones, etc. But no achievement, relationship, or image alteration can give us lasting esteem if we don't already claim it.

I used to constantly seek validation from friends and partners that I was smart, talented, and attractive. But it never lasted, because I didn't truly believe it myself deep down. I kept thinking I needed to improve myself or impress people to be worthy of love.

The truth is, I already was worthy simply by existing. We all are. Self-esteem isn't something we need to earn - our essential value is inherent. We just need to stop blocking it with judgment and limiting beliefs. Anything we do to raise self-esteem is really about uncovering its already existing presence within us.

Trying to pump ourselves up or censor undesirable traits doesn't work for long. Because those disowned parts are still there, now just festering in the shadows. Esteem based on denying or exaggerating facets of ourselves isn't holistic.

Lasting confidence comes from unconditionally accepting the wholeness and paradox of who we are - light and dark, strengths and weaknesses. It means knowing our essential worth persists no matter what we look like, accomplish, or fail at.

When we stop judging ourselves and clinging to ideals, what remains is a being deserving of love simply for existing. Releasing the need to prove our worth lets us relax into self-acceptance. We align with our inherent perfection, not an improved future version of ourselves.

Here are some signs you may be buying into the paradox of seeking self-esteem instead of claiming your inherent worth:

- You think you'll love yourself "when" you reach certain goals or milestones.

- Your confidence drastically rises and falls based on others' validation.

- You feel ashamed or anxious about expressing certain emotions or needs.

- You struggle to take compliments and praise yourself.

- You compare and judge yourself harshly against ideals or other people.

- You rely heavily on your looks, achievements, status, roles, etc. for esteem.

The paradox crumbles once we realize being worthy of love and belonging isn't something we gain - it's something we inwardly reclaim. We already are whole and complete as we are.

Here are some ways to start aligning with your inherent worth:

- Recognize every human has strengths and limitations - this equalizes us in our imperfect perfection.

- Let go of ideals you've judged yourself against or tried molding yourself to be.

- Accept that you already are lovable - it's not something you'll "get" later through achievements.

- Express all emotions and desires openly without shame or hesitation.

- Take time to appreciate yourself and all the ways you're already extraordinary.

- Surround yourself with people who affirm your inherent worth, not superficial traits.

- Do what nourishes your spirit - not what you think you "should" do to be worthy.

Bringing real confidence into our lives means tuning out external validation and turning within. We release judgments, ideals, and limiting beliefs. What remains, shining brightly beneath it all, is a being deserving of love simply for existing. A being complete as we are. Claim this. You already are it.

Facing Your Inner Darkness is the Key to Loving Yourself

Many of us try all sorts of ways to boost our self-esteem. We work on changing certain aspects of ourselves to be more likable. We avoid showing parts of us that feel unacceptable. We seek validation from others about our positive qualities. But these strategies offer only a superficial sense of self-worth - not true esteem.

Lasting self-esteem comes from self-acceptance. And to fully accept ourselves, we have to stop rejecting the parts of us we've hidden away in our shadows. Our "shadow" refers to those aspects of ourselves that we were conditioned to view as bad, dangerous, or unacceptable. As children, we quickly learn what earns approval vs judgment from our parents, peers, and society. Traits that get criticized or silenced get buried deep in our unconscious shadows.

But just because we hide them doesn't mean those parts disappear. Like banished children, they live on unseen, desperately waiting to be welcomed home. Imagine you scolded a child every time she got angry and called her mean. She'd quickly learn to suppress her anger, maybe even from herself, to gain your affection. But that fiery anger doesn't vanish - it gets stored in her shadow, warping her self-image.

We all have emotions, needs, talents, or desires that got shamed into our shadows. Yet they are still part of us, whether we acknowledge them or not. That's why trying to fix our self-esteem by tweaking our image or seeking validation falls short. =

Lasting confidence requires wholly accepting every aspect of who we are - light and dark. The parts of us we deny hold invaluable gifts we need for inner balance and wholeness. They want to help us, not hurt us, no matter how scary they seem.

I long struggled with low self-worth because I rejected parts of myself as unacceptable. I tried being a "good girl" who was always sweet, calm, and compliant. But that denied other aspects like my passion, sensuality, anger, and need for solitude. Of course those unexpressed parts didn't disappear. They built up useless shame and anxiety from being stuffed down. Only by compassionately uncovering them through inner work could I find self-love.

Owning our shadows allows us to be authentic, not carefully edited to meet expectations. We stop anxiously policing ourselves and chasing others' approval. We uncover our wholeness beyond any rigid self-image.

Here are some of the key benefits shadow integration provides:

- Releases shame and judgment about the parts of you conditioned to be "unacceptable."

- Allows you to compassionately embrace the full spectrum of who you are.

- Brings awareness to disowned needs, desires, and skills you're missing.

- Frees you from conforming to others' ideals by living your unique truth.

- Cultivates unconditional, holistic self-love beyond image, achievement, or traits.

- Reveals your core wholeness that exists beneath any masks, roles, or labels.

- Harmonizes disconnected aspects of self into an integrated, aligned sense of esteem.

The process of shadow work is much like cleaning out an old, cluttered attic. You gently sort through long forgotten contents, keeping what enriches your life and finding proper homes for the rest. What remains is a clear, spacious room you can freely move through. Similarly, when you compassionately unpack your psychological shadows, you regain energetic and emotional space. You access your natural radiance freed from the density of suppression and denial.

Here are some tips for integrating shadow aspects on your inner journey:

- Notice any shame, fear, or judgment around a trait, emotion, or desire. This signals a disowned shadow.

- Own this quality as a valid part of your wholeness, neither good nor bad.

- Release limiting beliefs created around rejecting this part of yourself.

- Explore what need or gift it carries rather than making it "wrong."

- Find healthy expressions for it to balance your overall personality.

- Share aspects of this shadow with those you trust for further healing.

- Have compassion for all the ways you learned to disown parts of your beautiful self.

Our shadows take patience, courage, and self-compassion to illuminate. But befriending our inner darkness is essential work for anyone seeking true self-esteem beyond ego ideals. We must care for and own all of ourselves in order to wholly love ourselves.

As Carl Jung wisely said: "One does not become enlightened by imagining figures of light, but by making the darkness conscious." Let your shadow work be the doorway to self-acceptance.

Facing Tests From Your Shadow Self

We all have a shadow - the part of ourselves we try to hide, deny, or suppress. This shadow is made up of raw, messy parts of being human that we deem bad or unacceptable, so we pretend they don't exist within us. But our shadow never disappears. It lies in wait, ready to emerge and test us when we least expect it.

Our shadows start taking form early in life as we learn to edit ourselves to gain love and approval. If we get scolded for throwing a tantrum, acting jealous, or crying from fear, we quickly start filtering out those "shameful" traits. We construct a polite, polished social mask and lock away anything that doesn't fit our ideal image.

But our hidden shadows still influence our perceptions and reactions. When we come across people exhibiting traits we've repressed in ourselves, it triggers intense emotions. Our unconscious shadows essentially "test" us through these charged encounters.

For example, say you consider yourself an exceptionally kind, ethical person. You value morality and compassion. Then you meet someone who you view as a cruel manipulator. You have a severe distaste and judgment about this person's immoral character.

Well, your intense condemnation likely exposes your own repressed shadows around moments of deceit, betrayal, or using others. We often fiercely reject traits in others that we can't tolerate knowing exist within. So this interaction "tests" you, bringing your unconscious shadows into awareness.

Or imagine you have a friend who constantly complains about her difficult life. She fixates on every challenge and seems to expect you to provide constant reassurance. You view her as a powerless victim who needs to take responsibility. You feel exhausted by her neediness.

In this case, your irritation reveals shadows around your own vulnerability and desire to feel validated or supported. her complaining touches a nerve, activating shadows you've repressed. So again, this relationship dynamically tests you.

Other common shadow tests include:

- Feeling contempt for someone's arrogance or pride can expose your denied insecurities and self-doubt. Their confidence triggers your shadows.

- Judging someone as lazy or undisciplined can reveal your repressed desires to relax, procrastinate, or self-indulge. Their lack of drive contrasts with your rejected slothful tendencies.

- Looking down on someone as melodramatic or emotional exposes shadows around suppressing your own hurt feelings or open expression. Their raw vulnerability contrasts with your contained shadows.

- Feeling irritation about someone's anger or hostility reveals shadows around being unable to honor your own boundaries or assertiveness. Their fierceness contrasts with your repressed fire.

Of course, sometimes people do exhibit genuinely annoying traits! But when you have an intense, judgmental reaction, that's the clue a repressed shadow has been triggered. Use these charged moments as opportunities for self-reflection. What is it about them that really gets under your skin? What might that say about hidden parts of yourself?

Now, we may still choose to keep our shadow traits private or expressed constructively. For instance, taking a brisk walk to cool anger versus exploding at someone. Or writing in a journal about jealousy versus undermining the person who evokes that insecurity.

Befriending Your Shadow

It's tempting to feel disgusted by our own hidden shadows. We don't want to acknowledge those unsavory parts exist within us. But shaming and hating our shadows will backfire. Remember, your shadow contains universal human experiences. Needing to rest, lacking confidence, feeling jealous or insecure - these are all normal from time to time.

Rather than judging yourself for those vulnerable traits, talk gently to your shadow like you would a friend in need. Don't call yourself pathetic for feeling depressed sometimes, but offer kind words of comfort instead. Don't berate yourself for getting irritated, but have compassion for the underlying hurt or stress. Keep your inner dialogue kind.

You might say: "I know you feel inadequate right now, but you are enough just as you are." Or "I understand you're afraid to speak up, but I believe in you and your voice matters." Speak to your shadow self as the hurting part of you that longs for wholeness and acceptance. Give it the patience and care you'd grant any struggling person.

While we can't let our shadows run rampant, we also shouldn't pretend they don't exist. Your messy humanness is nothing to be ashamed of. With compassion and courage, you can acknowledge your shadow traits without letting them define you completely. Say, "This feeling of jealousy doesn't make me a bad person. It simply shows I long for more connection or fulfillment."

Talk to your shadow with the wisdom that its emotions provide opportunities for growth, not cause for self-loathing. By befriending our shadows, we integrate disowned aspects of ourselves and become more whole. The result is greater self-awareness, authenticity, and peace.

The Mirror Effect

Have you ever noticed yourself judging someone harshly only to later realize you were actually projecting your own insecurities onto them? This phenomenon is known as psychological projection, and it's more common than you might think. Projection is a defense mechanism we all use to some degree, whether consciously or unconsciously. It allows us to externalize the parts of ourselves that feel too difficult or threatening to acknowledge.

Jung referred to these disowned aspects as our "shadow selves." We all have a shadow - those darker parts of ourselves that we'd rather reject and keep hidden. The problem is, the more we reject and suppress our shadow, the more it controls us from within, influencing our thoughts, feelings, and behaviors without us even realizing it.

This is where projection comes in. When we project, we unconsciously transfer the traits we can't accept in ourselves onto someone else. For example, if you have a strong fear of failure, you might regularly criticize your coworker for being "unmotivated" or "lazy," when in reality, it's your own fear and self-doubt that's making you lash out. Or, if you have insecurities around your appearance, you might harshly judge another woman for being "vain" or "shallow" because she likes fashion and makeup. When, deep down, you worry that you're not attractive enough yourself. Our ego does this to protect itself from pain or discomfort--it's easier to point the finger outward than admit that something inside ourselves needs attention or healing.

Projection allows us to see our own flaws reflected back at us without having to consciously face them. It's like a funhouse mirror that distorts our shadows and displays them externally. This "mirror effect" is why our reactions to others often say more about ourselves than them. The people who irritate or anger us the most tend to be those who reflect parts of ourselves we don't want to see.

The Shadow Work Connection

So how does the shadow possess us? Through projection. When we are unwilling to acknowledge the flaws and insecurities within, we project them outward onto other people. For example, if you experienced emotional neglect as a child, you may have stuffed a deep sense of unworthiness into your shadow. As an adult, you might regularly accuse your partner of not caring enough about you or prioritizing you when the feeling of neglect is actually coming from your own shadow.

Or, if you suffered from bullying or social rejection growing up, you might have buried a lot of anger and bitterness deep within. But this anger has to go somewhere, so you direct it outwards toward others in judgment or hostile criticism. Essentially, the people and situations that trigger you the most often reflect your repressed shadows. They hold up a mirror that you desperately want to avoid looking into.

The more we project our shadow material onto others, the more we distort our perceptions of reality. We start to see darkness everywhere except within. We become convinced that certain people or groups are inherently defective or dangerous, when we're really just seeing disowned parts of ourselves in them. Our unacknowledged inner demons get projected out into the world like demons possessing and controlling us.

The solution is shadow work: bravely confronting our inner darkness, taking back our projections, and reclaiming the lost parts of ourselves. This takes tremendous courage, brutal honesty with ourselves, and the willingness to face pain. But in Jung's words, "one does not become enlightened by imagining figures of light, but by making the darkness conscious." We can't transform our inner shadows without first acknowledging their existence.

Shadow work involves intentionally withdrawing energy from our projections and redirecting it inward for self-examination. We must trace our pain and fear back to their roots inside us, rather than blaming outward. This releases us from the grip of our shadows, so we can start integrating these denied aspects into our whole self. Then we can relate to others from a place of compassion instead of judgment, no longer tormented by our inner demons.

The journey is long, but the destination - wholeness and inner peace - is worth it. Our shadows, once embraced, can teach us more about ourselves and humanity than anything else. The parts of us we deem monstrous become our greatest teachers. It takes courage to love ourselves unconditionally, shadows and all. But it's the only way to stop projecting and reclaim our integrity. The light is found not by banishing darkness, but by gently illuminating it.

Finding Better Mirrors

The people in our lives often serve as mirrors, reflecting parts of ourselves back to us. Those who trigger us most tend to illuminate our hidden inner shadows - the flaws, wounds, and unhealed pain we try to reject. While these challenging relationships can aid our growth and self-discovery, surrounding ourselves only with negative mirrors can be draining and destructive. For true transformation, we must also seek out positive mirrors who call forth our highest potentials. Here are some tips on finding better mirrors and creating uplifting relationships:

1. *Evaluate your current relationships* - Which people create negative emotional reactions like anxiety, anger, or shame? These relationships likely reflect your shadow traits. On the flip side, which people make you feel uplifted, valued, and empowered? These are your positive mirrors.

2. *Initiate difficult conversations* - Talk honestly with negative mirrors about how the relationship makes you feel. Explain how their words/actions tap into your deeper insecurities. Give them a chance to adjust their behavior or apologize. If they remain toxic, you may need to detach.

3. *Watch for projection* - Remember that no person can be fully positive or negative. We all have light and dark within us. So beware of idealizing positive mirrors or demonizing negative ones. Projection distorts our view of reality.

4. *Withdraw energy from projections* - When you catch yourself projecting onto someone, withdraw energy from the projection and redirect it inward. Ask yourself, "What quality am I

seeing in this person that I need to develop in myself?"

5. *Embrace your disowned traits* - The negative mirrors in your life reflect the parts of yourself you've rejected and tossed into shadow. So those difficult relationships are opportunities to reclaim and integrate those denied aspects.

6. *Set boundaries* - You can still do shadow work with negative mirrors, but set clear boundaries to protect your energy. Limit time together and refrain from certain toxic topics/behaviors.

7. *Replace fantasies with reality* - Don't fantasize that your negative mirrors will magically transform into positive ones. Accept the healthy, realistic aspects of the relationship without projection or wishful thinking.

8. *Release resentment* - Forgive negative mirrors for reflecting parts of you that need work. Their unconscious mirroring is helping you heal and grow. Resentment distorts the mirror and keeps you stuck.

9. *Cultivate self-love* - The more you love yourself fully - shadows and all - the less you'll get tangled up in negative projections. You'll attract mirrors that affirm your true worth.

10. *Find mentors* - Seek out mentors who believe in you, share wisdom, and inspire growth. Their example can positively mirror back your own potential.

11. *Nurture new relationships* - As you heal old wounds, you'll naturally detach from negative mirrors and attract more positive ones. But also proactively cultivate relationships

with kind, supportive people.

12. *Give others the benefit of the doubt* - When someone irritates you, rather than demonize them, pause first. Reflect on how they could actually be an instrument for your growth if you respond with grace.

13. *Mirror positive qualities* - When you notice positive qualities in others, consciously reflect those qualities back to them through compliments and appreciation. Be a bright mirror.

14. *Express your needs kindly* - Tell positive mirrors how they can best support you in a considerate manner. Help them mirror your needs by expressing them clearly and without judgment.

15. *Offer forgiveness freely* - When positive mirrors fall short, forgive them readily so gratitude, not resentment, remains. Forgiveness nurtures relationships and helps us remember others' goodness.

As you do your inner work, you'll attract more positive mirrors over time. But you can also proactively seek out supportive mentors, friends, and partners. The right mirrors help you see your shadows without getting lost in darkness and recognize your own light. Keep transforming yourself, and your relationships will transform too.

Facing Your Shadow

We spend so much of life hiding our fears, running from our heartaches, and squashing down our anger, shame, and pain. In fact, we get so used to doing this that it becomes automatic. All of this denial creates huge roadblocks and repeated patterns.

There's a saying, "If you don't work it out, you'll act it out". So, all that stuff you've been burying doesn't stay buried. It's all there, in your subconscious, and will come to the surface again and again until you admit your truth. It takes a lot of courage to face your shadow, but imagine the possibilities once you do !ou'll be able to find all the peace, happiness, and success you've been looking for but could never find.

Most people never face their darker side though. They've either convinced themselves it doesn'treally exist or believe they can keep hiding from it. I can guarantee though, when you least expect it, when your defenses are down, or when life hits youwith an unwelcome surprise, it's going to leak out.

Typically, your shadow will sabotage you by taking the form of doubt, fear, distraction, orprocrastination any time you try to take a step up in life. Our shadow alsokeeps us stuck in unhealthy relationships and dead-end jobs, addictions, and along list of negative behaviors.

When your shadowsprings to the surface your emotions will always be out of proportion to thesituation. You'll feel intense rage, sadness, shame, hurt, or worry that's somuch bigger than the actual event you're currently facing. These explosiveemotions aren't necessarily bad, they're just trying to get your attention andlet you know that there are deeper issues to be worked on.

If we're honest withourselves we'll admit that it's exhausting to keep denying and hiding ourshadows. If we never face them, not only will we continually sabotage our bestefforts, but over the years, those toxic emotions can show up as physical painand disease.

The next time your shadow comes to the surface, rather than ignoring it or pushing it back down,use it as a chance to resolve long-ignored emotions and experiences. Once youget to the root cause and face it head-on you'll begin to heal. Your energywill be free, allowing you to finally live life as your authentic self.

The Roadmap to Inner Healing

Ignoring our shadows doesn't make them disappear. In fact, suppression only gives them more power over us. To find freedom, we must shine a light on our inner darkness. Shadow work provides a roadmap to heal and integrate the hidden aspects of ourselves. By courageously exploring our shadows, we can break free from their grip and step into our full authenticity. This journey requires dedication, self-love, and the willingness to face pain. But the rewards are immense: reclaiming lost soul fragments, relieving inner suffering, and relating to others from a place of wholeness rather than projection. Here are the key steps on the roadmap to inner healing through shadow work:

Self-Reflection

The work begins by pausing to reflect on our life experiences, relationships, and emotional patterns. We identify recurring triggers, conflicts, and periods of reactivity. These are clues pointing to our shadows. For example, if you frequently lash out when you feel rejected, you may have suppressed emotional wounds around abandonment. Reflection allows us to spot where our shadows leak out so we can investigate further. Here are some actionable steps for Self-Reflection:

- Carve out dedicated time for introspection, whether through journaling, meditation, or simply setting aside quiet moments for contemplation.

- Examine your relationships and emotional reactions - when do you feel yourself becoming unusually defensive, ashamed, or judgmental?

- Reflect on patterns in your life, such as recurring conflicts, feelings of dissatisfaction, or the types of people you're attracted to or repelled by.

- Consider events from your past that may have led you to suppress certain emotions or characteristics. What coping mechanisms did you develop?

- Bring a curious, non-judgmental attitude to this process. The goal is to observe, not criticize.

- Be patient with yourself. Uncovering our shadows can be a

gradual and sometimes uncomfortable process.

The key is to approach this self-reflection with an open mind, allowing yourself to become aware of the hidden parts of yourself that may be influencing your thoughts, feelings, and behaviors. This awareness is the first crucial step in the journey of shadow work and healing.

Cultivating Awareness

Next, we build awareness of our moment-to-moment thoughts, feelings, and behaviors. We tune into irrational impulses, knee-jerk reactions, projections, and other signs we're acting from the shadow. Developing this witnessing consciousness helps us catch our shadows in the act so we can take responsibility. Awareness breaks the spell of unconscious possession. Here are some steps for Cultivating Awareness:

- Practice mindfulness techniques, such as meditation or breathwork, to become more attuned to the present moment.

- Throughout your day, periodically pause and do a "body scan" - notice any sensations, emotions, or urges arising without judgment.

- Pay close attention to your reactions, especially in charged situations. What thoughts or feelings arise that don't seem proportional to the circumstances?

- When you notice a strong emotional response, take a moment to ask yourself, "What is this really about?" Look beneath the surface.

- Keep a journal to document your observations. Over time,

patterns may emerge that shed light on your shadow material.

- Be patient and compassionate with yourself. Cultivating awareness is a skill that takes practice.

The key is to approach this process with an attitude of curious, non-judgmental observation. By bringing awareness to our shadows, we break the unconscious cycle of reactivity and open the door to deeper understanding and integration.

Exploration

Now we actively explore our shadow material through journaling, therapy, meditation, or other inner work. We dig into past traumas and experiences we've repressed. We examine our secret fears and insecurities, uncovering the roots of shame. This requires radical self-honesty and letting go of denial. We get curious about the origins of our pain and the self-protective beliefs we formed to cope. Here are some steps for Exploration:

- Set aside dedicated time for inner exploration, whether through journaling, therapy sessions, or meditative practices.

- Reflect on experiences from your past that may have led to the formation of your shadow material. What wounds or traumas did you experience?

- Examine your secret fears, insecurities, and self-limiting beliefs. Where do these come from, and how have they shaped your behaviors and worldview?

- Practice radical self-honesty, letting go of any denial or resistance to fully facing your shadow material.

- Approach this exploration with a sense of curiosity and self-compassion, rather than judgment or criticism.

- Be patient with yourself, as uncovering and integrating shadow material can be a gradual and emotionally challenging process.

- Consider seeking the support of a trusted therapist or guide to help navigate this phase of shadow work.

The key is to approach this exploration with an open, curious, and courageous mindset. By delving into the depths of our shadow, we create the opportunity for profound personal growth and transformation.

Acceptance

As we shed light on the shadows, we practice meeting these rejected aspects with compassion. We accept that our shadows house valuable wisdom and hold potential gifts, once healed. Our shadows protected us at times and have profound lessons to teach us. Acceptance is not resignation - it's simply acknowledging and honoring all facets of ourselves, light and dark. By accepting our shadow, we allow ourselves to integrate these rejected parts of ourselves, and allow them to reveal their lessons to us. Here are the steps you can take for Acceptance:

- Reflect on the ways your shadow material has both harmed and helped you throughout your life. What purpose did it serve?

- Practice self-compassion when confronting your shadow aspects. Speak to yourself with the same kindness you would a dear friend.

- Visualize embracing your shadow self, welcoming it into your consciousness with openness and care.

- Write a letter to your shadow, expressing gratitude for its role in your journey and committing to continued integration.

- Consider rituals or symbolic acts (e.g., burning a journal entry) to signify your acceptance of this part of yourself.

- Be patient and persistent. Acceptance is an ongoing process, not a single destination.

The key is to approach your shadow with an attitude of respect, curiosity, and compassion. By fully accepting all aspects of yourself, you create the space for deep healing and personal transformation.

Integration

The final step is integrating the gifts of our shadows into our whole self. We modify dysfunctional behaviors rooted in shadow aspects. We start expressing formerly suppressed emotions in healthy ways. We uncover the golden teachings hidden in our shadows, instead of just the darkness. This integration allows us to live as our authentic, empowered selves, relating to others from wholeness rather than projection. Our demons become our greatest teachers. Here are some steps for Integration:

- Identify specific behaviors, habits, or ways of being that are tied to your shadow material and need to be transformed.

- Experiment with new, healthier ways of expressing emotions or impulses that you've previously suppressed.

- Reflect on the wisdom and life lessons hidden within your

shadow aspects. How can you apply these insights to your life?

- Consciously incorporate the gifts of your shadow into your daily life and decision-making.

- Consider creative outlets, such as art or writing, to channel the energy of your integrated shadow material.

- Be patient and compassionate with yourself as you navigate this dynamic process of integration.

- Celebrate your progress and acknowledge the courage it takes to embrace your whole self.

The key to this final step is to view your shadow not as something to be vanquished, but as a valuable part of your being that, when integrated, can unlock your greatest potential. Through this holistic integration, you can step into the fullness of your authentic self.

Shadow work is a challenging, lifelong path that leads to incredible freedom. By bravely diving into our inner darkness, we reclaim lost soul fragments, heal traumatic wounds from the past, and relate to others with empathy. The roadmap provides guideposts along the way, but our individual journey depends on our level of courage and commitment to whole-self acceptance. For those willing to illuminate their inner shadows, profound transformation lies ahead. But it starts with the first step: the willingness to look within.

Making Time For Shadow Work

Embarking on the path of shadow work requires dedication and routine practice. While an hour a day might seem overwhelming, even small windows of focused inner work can lead to profound shifts over time.

Begin by considering what schedule is sustainable for you. Can you realistically spend 10 minutes a day on shadow work? Early morning before distractions set in is ideal. Or perhaps 20 minutes on your commute home a few times a week? Choose regular times you can stick to when you're most clear-headed. Shadow work goes deep, so limit sessions to 30 minutes maximum. Longer and you risk mental exhaustion or being blindsided by intense emotions. Staying present gets difficult after extended inner excavation. You also need time afterwards to process and integrate before plunging back in.

Try closing your sessions with 10 minutes of journaling to record discoveries, then self-care to nurture yourself. Take a warm bath, sip tea, listen to calming music. Find what replenishes you. Don't immediately return to regular tasks. Give yourself space to realign.

Be mindful of your energy levels before starting. If you're stressed, sleep-deprived, or emotionally charged, wait for a better time. Shadow work can feel amplified when you're already depleted, which breeds discouragement. Replenish your reserves first.

Also know when to take a break. If you hit an extra turbulent patch, pause your sessions temporarily. And schedule regular one-week breaks every two to three months to integrate gains. Pushing relentlessly can backfire. Allow yourself to rest and absorb your progress. You may also notice your life feels more vibrant and joyful after periods of intense shadow work. Ride these peaks as long as they last before plunging back into the depths. Appreciate the fruits of your labor.

When ready to begin each session, spend a few minutes relaxing through meditation, yoga, nature sounds, or music. Anything calming. This stillness helps you gently enter your inner world without force or tension. Breathe slowly to invoke peace and patience.

Once you start examining your shadow, avoid knee-jerk reactions. Don't condemn what you see or quickly shove it back down into darkness. Meet your findings with compassion, detachment, and the willingness to understand. Simply observe without judgment, like watching leaves float down a stream.

Affirm that these inner parts don't define you. They're just fragmented pieces ready to be called home into wholeness. Breathe through urges to criticize them or beat yourself up. React with grace, not shame. You're on a journey of self-love, not further rejection.

Also release expectations around your progress. Some sessions will be profound. Others mundane. Both are important. Trust that each moment of inner work lights your path, even if you can't yet see. Just keep walking. Your commitment matters more than any single revelation.

Finally, keep an ongoing journal to record your travels. Writing integrates discoveries into your consciousness and tracks subtle inner shifts you'd otherwise miss. Plus, journaling after sessions helps process emotions before re-entering your routine.

Shadow work takes time, energy, and regular commitment. But few practices offer such deep rewards. Even minutes a day can reveal your shadows, your gifts, your wholeness.

The Gift of The Shadow

Our shadow selves act from a place of wanting to protect us, even if the methods are no longer helpful. The way your shadow protected you as a child likely doesn't serve you anymore as an adult. However, it continues operating in the same reactive ways, unless you bring conscious awareness to transform it.

It's true that emotions like sadness, anger, and fear have their place in our lives. The problem is that our shadow side doesn't understand when it's appropriate to feel and express them. It tends to blow things out of proportion, reacting with rage, tears, or paralyzing anxiety in situations where a more measured response would serve us better.

Alternatively, the shadow may cause us to shut down emotionally and internalize everything until it festers. Repressed emotions and unresolved pain only grow stronger in the darkness when left unaddressed.

Rather than judging these shadow emotions as bad or wrong, recognize that they come from a place of wanting to protect you. Ask yourself what purpose they serve and what positive intentions might be behind them.

For instance, anger often covers up hurt, sadness or vulnerability. It's a signal that a boundary has been crossed and you need to stand up for yourself. Fear puts us on high alert for potential threats and danger. Even seemingly negative emotions have a role to play in our lives when expressed consciously.

The shadow side developed as a child still lives within you. But you're no longer a helpless child. You have the power as an adult to integrate your shadow in healthy ways, rather than letting it control you.

It's tempting to think finding joy and freedom means changing outer circumstances - getting a better job, losing weight, making new friends. But the real keys to happiness and fulfillment lie hidden within the darkness of our shadow selves.

What past pains and traumas still affect you? Where did you feel hurt, rejected, or held back? Just acknowledging these formative experiences starts to shine a light of awareness to dissolve the shadow. Remind yourself that you were just a child back then, you're no longer a victim. Meet your pain with gentleness and compassion.

The shadow has become accustomed to operating behind the scenes, in the dark recesses of our psyches. When we have the courage to inquire within and get curious about our shadow side, we can begin transforming old patterns. Hidden gems can be found even in the muddy depths of our subconscious if we dare to look. Our shadow reveals where we have more growing and healing to do.

Rather than running from the shadow by keeping busy and distracted, turn towards it with radical self-acceptance. All parts of ourselves just want to be seen, heard and understood. Judgment or resistance only makes the shadow dig in its heels. The path forward is not to fight the darkness, but to embrace it with empathy and love.

When we acknowledge our shadow, we take away its power over us. Seeing it clearly robs it of control and gives us the opportunity to make new choices. With consciousness, the shadow becomes simply another part of the beautiful mosaic of who we are. In this light, it can be reintegrated to serve us, instead of driving us unconsciously.

The gift of our shadow is the wholeness it brings when embraced. The more we deny or reject the dark within ourselves, the more fractured we become. But by courageously exploring our inner darkness, we reclaim lost parts of our soul and restore blessings hidden in our shadows.

Uncovering Hidden Gifts Within Your Shadow

Shadow projections reveal our hidden gifts. What we admire in others is often a reflection of our own latent potentials. For instance, if you put musicians on a pedestal, convinced their talent makes them special, you may be projecting musical gifts that lie dormant within you.

We inflate others to appear above us because we minimize our own abilities. But we all have special talents and genius within us, even if we don't acknowledge them. Just as a musician's skill comes naturally to them, you likely have innate gifts that come easily which you dismiss as "no big deal."

Start noticing when you feel enthralled by someone else's positive traits. Ask yourself - where within me do these same qualities reside? Your self-image may obscure them, but they exist within you. By reclaiming disowned gifts as part of yourself, you expand your identity and esteem.

Owning Your Brilliance

Many of us downplay or undervalue our own talents and strengths. We explain away things that come easily as just who we are, not acknowledging our unique genius. Uncovering these denied gifts hidden in our shadows is key to owning our brilliance.

Are you a natural caregiver who intuitively knows how to comfort and support people when they're hurting? Do you have a knack for creating warm, beautiful spaces that feel like home? Have you always picked up foreign languages easily?

Whatever innate skills and talents you possess but dismiss as nothing special contain golden shadows waiting to be integrated. Start noticing any areas where you excel and ask yourself - have I minimized how gifted I am in this?

Rather than comparing yourself to others, reflect on your own natural abilities. What comes easily when you're in a state of flow? Where do you shine without trying because it's who you authentically are? These are clues to your shadow gifts.

As you reclaim disowned talents, you start fully owning your brilliance. Rather than explaining away what comes naturally, appreciate that you have special genius in these domains. Own that you are uniquely gifted - not better or worse than others, but with rare skills nonetheless.

When we deny our shadows, we fragment ourselves, believing we lack what others possess. But shining light on our hidden potentials restores lost parts of ourselves. Every positive quality we reintegrate expands our self-concept and actualization of our gifts.

Wholeness Through Shadow Integration

Integrating our shadow makes us whole - a fully realized person who embraces all we are without denial or projection. This includes talents and positive traits disowned in childhood. To become whole, we must uncover our hidden gems.

As children, many of us received messages that certain qualities were good while others were bad. We learned to reject parts of ourselves to gain love and acceptance. But this fractured us, creating inner division and conflict.

Reclaiming your shadow gifts heals this fragmentation. The parts of you that were denied contain beautiful potentials you need for wholeness. Let go of limiting self-images and get curious about your hidden powers.

What natural abilities did you showcase as a child but were discouraged from developing? What interests or talents bring you joy that you've dismissed as unimportant? These clues reveal gifts waiting to be unwrapped.

Allow yourself to shine bright in areas you've dimmed out of fear of standing out or being "too much." Give yourself permission to own all of your strengths and brilliance. Rather than inflating others, celebrate your own latent potentials coming out of the shadows.

As you welcome back lost parts of yourself, you gain newfound peace and confidence. Expressing your full talents gives meaning and purpose to your life. Embodying your hidden gifts allows your authentic self to fully emerge into the light. Your inner peace and self-esteem will change immediately for each traity ou re-own, embrace and love. These positive traits are said to be the shadow gift.

Healing the Past

We put great effort into detoxing our physical bodies through cleanses, fasts and healthy eating. But what about cleansing our souls? Our inner world holds all of our experiences - both nourishing and toxic. Detoxing the soul means identifying and releasing the fears, traumas and limiting beliefs that hold us back. Like any detox, it can be uncomfortable at first. But toxic emotions and pain trapped within our souls eventually poison the entirety of our lives if left unaddressed. We must find the courage to bring these shadows into the light where they can be healed.

Everything you've endured is stored within your soul's memories - from childhood wounds to recent letdowns. Over time, painful experiences build up and solidify into a heavy shadow that follows you through life. This inner burden of unresolved traumas, unexpressed emotions and fearful beliefs unconsciously dictates how you see the world and yourself. Almost everyone of us carries unconscious blockages that stunt their growth in subtle ways. You may self-sabotage, struggle with anxiety or depression, attract the same painful situations, or feel stuck in life without knowing why. These patterns all stem from the toxic shadow stuffed into the depths of your soul.

The shadow is composed of all the parts of yourself you've tried to avoid, deny or reject due to shame, guilt or judgment from society or your inner critic. But anything in your psyche that remains unacknowledged will only continue to haunt you and limit your potentials. Bringing awareness to your shadow is the first step in a deep soul cleanse. Rather than pretending past pains didn't happen or minimizing their impact, allow yourself to fully feel and process these old wounds. This takes radical honesty, courage and compassion towards yourself.

It's tempting to deny having demons or keep painful memories locked away. No one wants to feel flawed or relive vulnerabilities. However, what you resist and repress gains more power over you in the darkness. Shedding light on your shadow is the only way to dismantle its control. Be patient with yourself if you don't feel ready yet to face certain traumas or insecurities head on. But know that your shadow will keep rising up through triggers and unconscious behaviors until you finally acknowledge its messages. These recurring signals are invitations to free yourself at last.

Once you've consciously acknowledged the existence of your inner demons, you can begin the work of releasing them through processing, expressing and integrating these shadows. This requires bravely confronting painful emotions you've expertly avoided thus far. Lean into therapeutic tools like journaling, counseling, grief rituals or trusted confidants to help heal old wounds as they surface. Though it may feel like reopening past scars, clearing out this toxic residue will leave you feeling renewed.

Picture your soul like a cluttered closet full of things you've outgrown but haven't discarded. You must empty out the closet before you can fill it with new, life-giving things. Similarly, clearing your shadows creates space for you to thrive.

Releasing toxic patterns also requires vigilance even after doing initial healing work. Old habits die hard, and your mind will try to pull you back into familiar ruts. Stay present and redirect yourself whenever you notice past traumas reemerging. With consistent practice, these painful memories will lose their charge and grip over you. In their place, previously blocked potentials can come forth. You'll gain newfound confidence, purpose and freedom to create the life you truly desire.

Detoxing your soul takes dedication, but the rewards are profound. Imagine how much energy you'll free up when you're no longer carrying old burdens or being driven by unconscious fears. By courageously diving into your inner shadows, you'll reclaim lost parts of your radiant soul. You'll no longer be haunted or defined by your past. Your entire being will feel lighter and more vibrant. When left unaddressed, the shadow consumes all that you are. But by illuminating and releasing it, you reclaim your wholeness. The void left behind inspires you towards your highest potentials.

Healing the Shadow

Healing the shadow means welcoming back these disowned aspects and accepting them as part of who we are. Integrating the shadow is the path to wholeness.

We all have a shadow composed of the elements of ourselves that we judge as negative or incompatible with how we wish to be seen. We instinctively want to reject or repress whatever doesn't fit into our idealized identity. But anything we cast out doesn't actually go away – it just gets stuffed into our shadow.

From there, the shadow continues to affect our lives, driving behaviors and patterns outside of our awareness. We remain fragmented, believing we "lack" certain qualities others seem to possess. The shadow essentially controls us from behind the scenes, since we refuse to acknowledge its presence.

Bringing our shadows into conscious awareness is what allows us to integrate them in a healthy way. This requires taking an honest look within to uncover times when the shadow aspects were present. The goal is not to judge ourselves for them, but simply accept they are part of the human experience.

For example, reflect on instances when you acted selfishly in the past. Without any self-blame, acknowledge that some degree of selfishness exists within you, as it does in all people. Make space for it as an inevitable part of life.

Through this radical self-acceptance, we no longer need to expend energy denying or repressing the parts of us that feel unacceptable. We heal as we withdraw the power we've given to the inner critic that judges and rejects our shadow.

Reintegrating traits back into your self-concept returns you to wholeness. You reclaim fragmented parts of your psyche that had been cast away, making you more at peace with all that you are. Your self-esteem grows as you unconditionally embrace yourself.

The more you welcome back the shadow, the less it controls you. Taking charge of your inner world helps you become the author of your own life story, instead of living reactively. You move through the world with full authentic empowerment.

This inner work is ongoing, as there are always more layers to unfold. But each small act of befriending your shadow grants you greater alignment, joy and sense of purpose. You come home to yourself as you honor all that lies within.

Rather than living in a state of conflict with yourself, you move through life with an integrated wholeness.

Embracing Wholeness

Healing the shadow is about reclaiming these traits that you project onto others. The shadow of our psyche has within it huge potential for growth and getting your life back on track. This process of radical self-acceptance allows us to become whole. Here are steps to start integrating your shadow:

1. Identify Your Blind Spots

Make a list of all the qualities and traits you believe you possess, both positive and negative. Be radically honest with yourself here - don't just list the idealized identity you wish you had. Then, reflect on your blind spots - areas where you lack self-awareness about behaviors or patterns. What negative tendencies or reactions are you quick to justify or excuse away? These blind spots provide entry points to uncover your shadow aspects. For example, maybe you view yourself as patient and kind, but fly off the handle when someone cuts you off driving. Road rage reveals anger living in your shadow. Or you see yourself as selfless, yet resentment builds when you don't get appreciated. Closely examine any inner conflicts between who you think you are versus how you actually behave at times. Lean into discomfort to shed light on blind spots. This illuminates pathways into your shadow.

2. Uncover Projections

Beyond blind spots, projections reveal unknown aspects of your shadow. For a referesher on this, refer to Chapter 8: The Mirror Effect.

Pay close attention to what irritates, repulses or provokes strong reactions in you when interacting with others. The things you strongly dislike or judge in another person often reflect disowned parts of yourself that you're projecting onto them. For instance, if you have an especially hard time tolerating arrogant or "know-it-all" types, you may be externalizing and disowning your own arrogance or smugness. If you despise cruel people, cruelty lives somewhere in your shadow. Or if you seethe with resentment when others breeze through life rewarded for minimal work while you struggle and grind, you're likely disowning your own laziness and desire for ease. Remember that we all contain the full spectrum of human potentials within us, but often can only see it in others. What you can't bear or rubs you the wrong way in someone else can clue you into your shadow. Lean into discomfort and be radically honest with yourself as you uncover these projections. This illuminates gold hidden in your shadow.

3. Get Curious, Not Critical

Once you've started to uncover your shadow aspects through blind spots and projections, it's vital to approach these discoveries with openness and compassionate curiosity rather than criticism or judgment. Remind yourself that your shadow is not some enemy or bad part of you, but simply the accumulation of unacknowledged parts of yourself that want to be welcomed back home. From a place of gentleness, get curious about why these shadow traits developed in the first place. How did they protect or benefit you at one time? What past experiences or childhood wounds caused you to disown certain qualities and bury them away? Are the roots based in trauma, family dynamics, or societal conditioning?

Understanding where your shadow originated allows you to see the inherent innocence and goodness even in the parts of you that seem dark. And remember that all humans, even the most enlightened masters, have a shadow composed of the full spectrum of human qualities and tendencies. Become fascinated with this dimension of your inner world. The more open and curious you are, the more your shadow will reveal its gifts to you. Judgment causes the shadow to retreat even deeper.

4. Find the Roots

An important part of shadow integration is tracing when these qualities first emerged for you or identifying key experiences that caused you to reject and disown certain traits. Were there childhood traumas, dysfunctional family patterns, or emotional wounds that shaped which aspects you embraced and which you buried away? For instance, if you disown and repress rage, reflect on how expressing anger was discouraged or punished when you were young. If you deny issues with control, consider how powerlessness or lack of security in childhood made you disown more dominant shadow aspects. Or if you minimize your talents and strengths, look at how pursuing excellence led to painful criticism from a parent.

Really make the links between your past and what lives in your shadow currently. Some shadows even originate from past lives or ancestral patterns embedded in your psyche before this lifetime. Understanding the roots allows you to develop empathy and compassion for why you learned to push certain pieces of yourself into the dark. And it reminds you that those experiences happened long ago to a vulnerable child, not your present self. You're now ready to reclaim the pieces you disowned and become whole.

5. Accept All That You Are

With greater awareness of your shadow, the next step is a practice of radical self-acceptance of all that you are. Remind yourself that every quality and trait that is possible in human nature exists within you - that's simply the reality of being human. For instance, we all have some degree of darkness and light, love and hate, fear and courage, self-ishness and generosity. No one area dominates your true nature. But because of past experiences causing us to disown parts of ourselves, we fragment and believe we "lack" certain qualities that others possess. Integrating your shadow is about returning to a state of wholeness where you unconditionally accept the full spectrum of who you are.

Make it a daily practice to consciously accept and embrace those shadow aspects you are beginning to uncover. You might look in the mirror and say "I accept my arrogance", "I accept my laziness", "I accept my cruelty." This act of conscious acceptance takes their power away. They no longer need to be controlled or denied. As you welcome all that you are, those lost fragments can be rewoven into the wholeness of your being.

6. Integrate Your Shadow

Once you've brought shadow aspects into conscious awareness through uncovering your blind spots, projections and past roots, you can start the process of actually welcoming them back and re-integrating them into your sense of self in a healthy way. This requires you to withdraw the energy you've put into judging, repressing or controlling these qualities, often fueled by the inner critic. If you try to destroy or cut off your shadow, it will only come back stronger until you acknowledge it with compassion. So be the observer of these parts of you rather than trying to manipulate them. Say internally "I recognize this exists within me and now allow it to integrate." Be patient with stumbles as there is often two steps forward, one step back.

Over time as you relax the unnecessary inner conflict, your shadow will take up less space and be less likely to control you reactively. You'll gain more access to its gifts. Integration leads to wholeness. But make sure to take regular emotional release breaks when needed - this is intense inner terrain! Having support like a therapist or teacher is also invaluable.

7. Release Control

A vital mindset shift for shadow integration is accepting that you do not need to be one static way. Humans are ever-changing and life is in flux, so the aspects that make up your mosaic self will vary too. Give yourself permission to be a complex, multifaceted being. You cannot grip tightly around having a fixed identity or always being a certain way. Attempting to do so will only breed inner conflict and suffering. For example, if you view yourself as someone who is always kind and patient, yet impatience and frustration begin arising, you'll judge those feelings as unacceptable and try to repress them back into the shadow, causing more division within yourself.

If you allow those shadow aspects space to exist when they naturally arise, without spiraling into self-attack, they lose destructive power and can be constructively channeled. You don't have to be a saint or completely perfect all the time in order for the shadow to be integrated. In fact, perfectionistic ideals often breed shadow aspects. Releasing control around how you believe you need to appear even internally is incredibly liberating. Your experience of life will ebb and flow, as will the traits that come forward. You've got this!

8. Keep Exploring Layers

Healing and integrating your shadow is not a one-and-done process, but rather a continuous journey that unfolds over a lifetime. We all have many layers to our inner worlds. Just when you feel you know yourself deeply, a new undercurrent will reveal itself over time. Life events also shape and shift our sense of self and bring different elements of the shadow to light. The work occurs in spirals, with themes coming up repeatedly each round but with opportunity to transmute them at deeper levels. You build self-awareness like strengthening a muscle. While the initial layers you uncover may feel more intense and charged, the deeper realms of the shadow often contain great gifts once brought to light. Some choose to devote themselves to lifelong inner excavation through deep therapeutic work, meditation, dream analysis, etc. Not only does this benefit your own wellbeing, but it brings more consciousness to the collective.

Tread with care, patience and self-compassion on the journey. You may stumble upon personal or ancestral wounds that are best opened with support. Build a team of guides like therapists, teachers and friends to assist at challenging times. Know that the path has endless riches when you commit to keep digging. But remember, the point isn't perfection, rather wholeness through embracing all that you find within.

When you reject parts of yourself, it causes inner division and conflict. Integrating your shadow restores you to wholeness. The more you welcome back the disowned aspects, the less the shadow controls you.

Practical Approaches to Shadow Work

Shadow work involves illuminating the unknown parts of ourselves and integrating them into our awareness. This inner exploration leads to wholeness and healing. While the work of uncovering our shadows takes commitment and bravery, the rewards outweigh the discomfort. We release old wounds, limiting beliefs and trapped emotions. This clears space for greater joy, fulfillment and connection.

When we deny parts of ourselves, we suffer and struggle unconsciously. But shining light into the darkness of our inner world returns us to wholeness. There are many paths into the depths within. With care, we are able to slowly unravel the stories, memories and experiences written in our shadows. This hidden treasure waits patiently to be found.

While the journey is deeply personal, there are practical tools to uncover and understand our shadow aspects. Here, we will discuss some of the diverse techniques to gently bring our shadows into conscious awareness.

Journaling and Reflective Writing

Journaling provides a pathway to illuminate our shadows through unfiltered self-reflection and expression. Putting our inner experiences into words externalizes what lives within us. This process unravels the unconscious terrain that shapes our lives.

Writing in a journal creates space to acknowledge parts of ourselves that we typically avoid or deny. We give form to emotions, memories, dreams, fears - anything emerging from our subconscious. The words on the page bring clarity to our inner world.

Journaling sheds light on blind spots, projections, and inner conflicts. We can track patterns, gain insights into motivations behind our behaviors, and give voice to disowned aspects of ourselves begging to be addressed. This builds self-awareness and compassion.

By releasing inner blockages through writing, we create space for our shadows to transform. Putting our shadows into language integrates them into our consciousness where they can be healed.

Here are some steps to begin journaling for shadow work:

- Set a regular time to write freely without editing yourself

- Use prompts like "What am I feeling but afraid to admit?"

- Write stream-of-consciousness without self-judgment

- Read back past entries to notice themes and growth

- Dialogue with different aspects of yourself on paper

- Visualize negative emotions flowing out through your pen

While discomfort may arise, journaling provides a safe container to explore the shadow's messages. There are often gems of wisdom waiting to be found in our darkest places within.

Through consistent journaling, we unpack old wounds, limiting beliefs and trapped emotions. We reconnect with disowned parts of ourselves, returning to wholeness. Our inner world illuminates.

Dream Analysis and Interpretation

Dreams speak the language of the subconscious and reveal unknown parts of ourselves. Analyzing our dreams can shed light on emotions, desires and shadows that our waking minds repress.

While dreaming, the ego's defenses are lowered. Our inner world comes to life unfiltered as our conscious mind sleeps. Dreams expose powerful symbols, stories, and messages from our shadows.

By reflecting on dreams, we can uncover recurring themes, buried memories, and inner conflicts that hold us back. What we avoid facing by day arises cloaked symbolically by night, waiting to be unveiled.

Noticing patterns in dreams over time provides clues to where our attention is needed for inner healing and integration. Keeping a dream journal supports this shadow work.

Here are some tips to interpret dreams:

- Upon waking, immediately record dreams in detail

- Notice emotions and physical sensations within the dream

- Reflect on symbols and your associations with them

- Look for connections to waking life problems or relationships

- Discuss dreams with a therapist or experienced guide

- Use meditation and creative practices to understand their

messages

While dreamwork requires patience and practice, it grants access to the riches of our subconscious inner life. Our shadows speak volumes if we learn their language. and over time we can metabolize the full spectrum of our inner world revealed through dreams. This brings greater alignment, joy and inner peace.

Psychoanalytic Techniques and Therapy

Seeking professional support through psychotherapy is invaluable when doing the intense work of shadow integration. Therapists offer tools to safely illuminate the unconscious parts of ourselves. Psychoanalytic therapy is specifically designed to bring awareness to the shadow. Methods include dream analysis, free association, transference interpretation and holding the psyche's projections.

Having an experienced guide provides perspective when deeply exploring our inner terrain. The shadow contains traumatic memories or painful emotions that can feel overwhelming to metabolize alone. Therapists help us build self-compassion, unravel recurring thought patterns, identify childhood wounds, and understand the messages of our shadows. Their support helps us integrate what we discover.

Some key benefits of exploring the shadow with a therapist:

- A safe space to express the full spectrum of yourself

- Guidance interpreting dreams, projections and inner dynamics

- Support through emotional triggers and old pain arising

- Accountability to stay committed to the work

- Skills to healthily embody and integrate your shadows

- A witness to your transformation who affirms your progress

While the presence of a therapist creates space for our shadows to emerge, this is deep internal work that also requires dedication on our part. Together a therapeutic alliance can illuminate our inner darkness, releasing us into wholeness.

Having a professional guide provides the courage to face the shadows we all carry within our hearts. With skilled support, we can explore even our most troubling inner demons, reclaiming the fragmented pieces of our souls in a safe envrionment. We remember we are not alone on the journey.

Art and Creative Expression

Artistic and creative expression allow our shadows to emerge in uncensored ways. Bypassing the rational mind's constraints, our inner world flows onto the page, canvas or stage. Practices like art-making, dance, music, poetry and drama give form to the shapeless unconscious realm within. We translate our shadows into tangible expression.

The spontaneity of creation lets hidden emotions, buried memories and neglected aspects of self come forward. What we avoid seeing clearly arises in symbolic form through images, sounds and movement. As we give material existence to our inner shadows, we can observe them with compassion rather than clinging to old judgments. Art illuminates our wholeness.

Here are some ways to explore your shadow creatively:

- Paint or draw images from your dreams or imagination

- Write stream-of-consciousness poetry to express your raw feelings

- Move your body freely to music to release stuck energies

- Take photographs that represent different parts of your psyche

- Sculpt or mold clay into forms that depict your contradictions

- Embody your shadow through dramatic role-play and theater

Trust your intuition and allow your inner wisdom to guide the art-making process. Don't judge the result.

Creative shadow work reveals new perspectives. It connects us to our buried emotions, memories, desires and disconnects. We reintegrate estranged pieces of ourselves. When we give tangible form to our inner shadows, we no longer fear the darkness. We reconnect with the light of full self-understanding. Our creative spirit heals.

Mindfulness and Meditation Practices

Mindfulness and meditation cultivate conscious awareness and presence. These practices illuminate our shadows in the light of understanding. A vital step in shadow integration is nonjudgmental observation of our moment-to-moment experience. Mindfulness allows us to witness the workings of our psyche without identified with or clinging to them.

Noticing sensations, thoughts, and emotions with open curiosity, we recognize the shadow aspects we typically ignore or deny. By carefully observing rather than reacting, we detach their power over us. Meditation helps settle our busy minds, creating space for self-reflection. Silencing the chattering ego allows our shadows to subtly emerge into our awareness, waiting to be addressed.

Here are some mindfulness practices to reveal your shadow:

- Observe your stream of consciousness during meditation

- Bring mindful attention to daily activities and bodily sensations

- Notice emotional triggers and their connection to past
  wounds

- Identify negative self-talk and limiting beliefs as they occur

- Ask "What am I resisting or avoiding seeing in myself?"

- Journal reflectively about your experiences with nonjudg-
  ment

The light of mindfulness illuminates our unconscious beliefs, pains and patterns. It supports the integration of our shadows.

While shadows may initially feel louder when made conscious, continuing awareness practice helps dissolve their control over us. We regain choice over our actions. By mindfully unfurling our inner world, we uncover the roots of suffering and disconnection. This allows our shadows to be digested and released.

Psychodrama

Psychodrama utilizes guided dramatic action methods and role-playing to reveal our unconscious shadows. By acting out different parts of our psyche, we gain insight into ourselves. In psychodrama, participants dramatize internal conflicts, relationships issues, dreams, or past scenes from their lives. A facilitator helps set the stage and direct the action.

Taking on various roles gives voice to the different parts of ourselves. We bring to life our inner critic, our wounded inner child, a traumatic memory, or a lost loved one. Seeing these shadow aspects played out physically and psychologically makes them more tangible. New perspectives emerge when we step into different roles.

Here's how psychodrama can facilitate shadow work:

- Warm up with theater games to loosen inhibitions

- Determine a conflict or inner dynamic to dramatize

- Cast group members as key roles and set the scene

- Improvise dialogues and actions between roles

- Reverse roles to gain each perspective

- Share insights afterward on what surfaced for you

By dramatizing our inner world, we externalize psychic forces working beneath the surface. Our shadows become accessible. Psychodrama provides a powerful toolkit for uncovering and integrating disowned aspects of the self. We infuse our shadows with creativity and joy.

Emotional Release Practices

Emotional release practices help unlock feelings trapped in the body and psyche, providing a cathartic clearing for shadow work. When difficult emotions like shame, anger or grief remain unexpressed, they stagnate in the shadows. Releasing these blocked feelings brings light.

Cathartic vocalization, breathing techniques, physical exercises, and trauma-informed bodywork can dislodge stuck emotions safely. Guidance is recommended when intense shadows surface. Emotional release allows us to discharge painful, dense energy we carry from past trauma and repression. This makes space to integrate those aspects.

Here are some emotional release approaches:

- Cathartic vocalization - making spontaneous sounds to freely express emotions

- Rhythmic breathing - using connected breathing to release stuck feelings

- Physical exercise - moving the body vigorously to help emotions surface

- Bodywork - massage and therapies to unlock somatic holding patterns

- Ecstatic dance - undirected dance to release energy through movement

- Artistic expression - using creative arts to externalize inner emotions

- Destruction rituals - symbolically destroying objects representing negative emotions

Focus on sensing where emotions feel blocked in your body. Breathe into these places while making sound, moving, or engaging creatively to facilitate release. Emotional release work clears dense energetic blockages that obscure our inner light. Our shadows transform when directly expressed. As we uncork bottled up emotions, we reconnect with aspects of ourselves that became estranged. Our shadows are welcomed back home.

Final Thoughts: Shadow Work Changes Over Time

Shadow work is a deeply personal process that evolves as you heal and grow. When you first start exploring your inner darkness, the experience is new and intense. But if you stick with it over time, you'll notice the way you approach shadow work changes. After awhile, you aren't the same person anymore. You've already uncovered layers of repressed emotions, shed light on old wounds, and learned things about yourself. So when you sit down to do more shadow work, it feels different. The shadows look different in the light of your new perspective.

As you go deeper into the shadows, uncovering more of the parts of yourself you've tried to hide away, there's often an urge to run back into the light. None of us likes facing the uncomfortable feelings we find lurking there. Our first instinct is usually to get judgmental about it. We tell ourselves things like, "Why am I still holding onto this old memory? It's so small and insignificant! I should just get over it already."

I totally understand those judgmental reactions. I've been there too. Let me tell you about a memory that came up for me during shadow work that at first seemed silly to still be holding onto.

I was about ten years old and playing outside my cousin's house. I looked up and saw my mom driving away with my sister, and I completely freaked out. I went running and screaming after the car, begging her to stop. She did stop, but told me to stay and play. She said she'd be right back after getting food for everyone.

Little ten-year-old me was convinced in that moment that she was abandoning me for good. I cried and felt so afraid and alone until she came back, just like she said she would.

Of course, looking back now as an adult, I can see how overly dramatic my reaction was. My mom obviously came right back - it wasn't actually abandonment. So why did I react so strongly? At first, I felt embarrassed about it and wanted to just shove the memory away.

But here's the thing: those young, wounded parts of us don't change or grow up. My ten-year-old self still felt exactly the same terror and heartbreak in that moment. So why was I judging her so harshly for it? She had every right to feel afraid based on other experiences I'd had.

So I took a gentler look at that memory. I let it unfold and really felt all the overwhelming emotions instead of resisting them. I acknowledged that yes, my mother had abandoned me in other ways throughout childhood, so of course little me would feel terrified of it happening again. My fear was valid.

When I stopped shaming my younger self and just listened to her and comforted her, that memory lost some of its sharp, painful edges. It didn't disappear completely, but it softened.

We're only human. As we go through life, we experience traumatic things. Depending on our existing inner wounds, we either hold onto those experiences or let them go. Each time I felt abandoned or worried I might be, it added another layer to my shadow around abandonment. Over years, it grew thicker and more painful.

Simply acknowledging I have a fear of abandonment isn't enough to heal it. I've had to gently peel back each layered memory over time and give it the care and attention it needs.

Of course, some memories go so far back or are buried so deep, we may never uncover them all fully. That's okay. As long as you work with whatever does surface, you'll eventually integrate those shadow pieces.

The key is to approach your inner darkness with compassion, not judgment. If you can, just observe the memories and feelings without resistance. Immerse yourself in them. What do they have to say? What can they teach you?

The raw emotions you find in the shadows are honest reflections of how you truly felt - and maybe still feel. This is why shadow work takes commitment. Just when you think you've found the root cause, you dig deeper and uncover something else.

Remember that shadow work involves gradually confronting and healing the painful parts of yourself that you've tried to repress. When done with compassion, this process can lead to profound growth and inner peace. But how exactly do you do shadow work when those dark emotions surface? Each time you encounter one of these fragments, your job is to:

Identify the Roots

The first step is noticing when a shadow emotion arises and identifying where it's coming from. Pay attention to situations or experiences that trigger uncomfortable reactions like anger, fear, sadness, or disgust. These reactions indicate an old wound or insecurity lurking in your subconscious.

By tuning into the associated memory or belief, you can start uncovering the roots of your shadow. Sometimes they arise from a specific event in your past. Other times, they develop from ongoing emotional patterns or dynamics, like feeling unloved or unseen as a child. Shed light on the origins without judgment.

Accept with Compassion

Once you've shined a light on a shadowy part of yourself, the next step is acceptance. Know that this emotion served a purpose in your past as a protective mechanism. Although it feels unpleasant now, it holds value just like any other part of you.

Rather than rejecting or being disgusted by your shadows, consciously accept them with compassion. Doing so allows you to take ownership and responsibility for these feelings, rather than letting them control you unconsciously. Send love to the wounded inner child that needed this coping strategy.

Integrate with Understanding

Acceptance breaks down the barriers between you and your shadows. The next phase is integration. By embracing these emotions with understanding, you allow them to evolve in healthy ways.

Make space for difficult feelings without suppressing them. Listen to what they are trying to tell you. Integrate them into the wholeness of who you are, rather than hiding them away in shame.

Keep Revisiting with Patience

Shadow work is a gradual, lifelong process - not something you can do just once and consider complete. Emotions may arise again and again as you deepen self-discovery. When familiar shadows pop up, don't get frustrated. This just signals there are more layers to peel back and heal in that area.

Shadow work is an ongoing journey of self-discovery and growth. With time and patience, you'll find that facing your shadows becomes less and less daunting. The power they once held over you gradually diminishes as you continue to confront and integrate them over time. However, it's important to understand that inner growth is a lifelong process without a definitive endpoint. Revisiting your shadows with compassion remains crucial as you progress on your path of awakening.

Each time you engage in shadow work, you may uncover new insights or reprocess aspects you thought you had already resolved. If a particular issue resurfaces, view it as an opportunity to delve deeper into that shadow aspect rather than feeling frustrated by its persistence. Remember, healing is not always linear. Some shadows may require multiple encounters before they're fully integrated. You'll recognize true healing when a once-troubling aspect no longer holds the same emotional charge or influence over your thoughts and behaviors.